SEAWEED

Edible

Series Editor: Andrew F. Smith

EDIBLE is a revolutionary series of books dedicated to food and drink that explores the rich history of cuisine. Each book reveals the global history and culture of one type of food or beverage.

Already published

Apple Erika Janik *Banana* Lorna Piatti-Farnell
Barbecue Jonathan Deutsch and Megan J. Elias
Beef Lorna Piatti-Farnell *Beer* Gavin D. Smith
Brandy Becky Sue Epstein *Bread* William Rubel
Cake Nicola Humble *Caviar* Nichola Fletcher
Champagne Becky Sue Epstein *Cheese* Andrew Dalby
Chillies Heather Arndt Anderson *Chocolate* Sarah Moss
and Alexander Badenoch *Cocktails* Joseph M. Carlin
Curry Colleen Taylor Sen *Dates* Nawal Nasrallah
Doughnut Heather Delancey Hunwick *Dumplings* Barbara Gallani
Edible Flowers Constance L. Kirker and Mary Newman
Eggs Diane Toops *Fats* Michelle Phillipov *Figs* David C. Sutton
Game Paula Young Lee *Gin* Lesley Jacobs Solmonson
Hamburger Andrew F. Smith *Herbs* Gary Allen *Honey* Lucy M. Long
Hot Dog Bruce Kraig *Ice Cream* Laura B. Weiss *Lamb* Brian Yarvin
Lemon Toby Sonneman *Lobster* Elisabeth Townsend
Melon Sylvia Lovegren *Milk* Hannah Velten *Moonshine* Kevin R. Kosar
Mushroom Cynthia D. Bertelsen *Nuts* Ken Albala *Offal* Nina Edwards
Olive Fabrizia Lanza *Onions and Garlic* Martha Jay
Oranges Clarissa Hyman *Pancake* Ken Albala
Pasta and Noodles Kantha Shelke *Pie* Janet Clarkson
Pineapple Kaori O' Connor *Pizza* Carol Helstosky
Pomegranate Damien Stone *Pork* Katharine M. Rogers
Potato Andrew F. Smith *Pudding* Jeri Quinzio *Rice* Renee Marton
Rum Richard Foss *Salad* Judith Weinraub *Salmon* Nicolaas Mink
Sandwich Bee Wilson *Sauces* Maryann Tebben *Sausage* Gary Allen
Seaweed Kaori O'Connor *Soup* Janet Clarkson
Spices Fred Czarra *Sugar* Andrew F. Smith *Tea* Helen Saberi
Tequila Ian Williams *Truffle* Zachary Nowak
Vodka Patricia Herlihy *Water* Ian Miller
Whiskey Kevin R. Kosar *Wine* Marc Millon

Seaweed

A Global History

Kaori O'Connor

REAKTION BOOKS

Published by Reaktion Books Ltd
Unit 32, Waterside
44–48 Wharf Road
London N1 7UX, UK
www.reaktionbooks.co.uk

First published 2017

Printed and bound in China by 1010 Printing International Ltd

A catalogue record for this book is available
from the British Library

ISBN 978 1 78023 753 4

Contents

Introduction

Neither plant nor animal
I cover the globe but am rarely seen,
I sway with the wind,
But cannot stand on land,
People eat and use me every day
Without knowing it
Food of the past, food of the future
What am I?

The answer to this riddle is –
seaweed, the first superfood.

On our blue planet, oceans cover 71 per cent of the globe's surface.[1] Driven by a growing awareness of the limitations of land resources, the search for new foods, pharmaceuticals and other products is turning to the sea, and to seaweeds – the world's last great renewable natural resource and a culinary treasure ready for rediscovery.

In 1833, arriving at Tierra del Fuego at the foot of South America on HMS *Beagle*, the young naturalist Charles Darwin was struck by the richness of the surrounding sea which seethed with giant kelp and marine life, writing in his journal:

The number of living creatures of all Orders, whose existence intimately depends on the kelp, is wonderful . . . On the leaves [were] molluscs and bivalves. Innumerable crustacean frequent every part of the plant . . . I can only compare these great aquatic forests . . . with the terrestrial ones in the inter-tropical regions. Yet if in any country a forest was destroyed, I do not believe nearly so many species of animals would perish as here, from the destruction of the kelp. Amidst the leaves of this plant, numerous species of fish live, which nowhere else could find food or shelter; with their destruction the numerous cormorants and fishing birds, the otters, seals and porpoises, would soon perish also; and lastly the Fuegians [the people of Tierra del Fuego] . . . would decrease in numbers and perhaps cease to exist.[2]

Here, Darwin glimpsed a great natural law that is only now beginning to be appreciated – one way and another, much depends on seaweed.

What is Seaweed?

Seaweeds, a marine form of algae, are found in all the earth's oceans, in all climate zones from the warm seas of the tropics to the cold waters of the Arctic and Antarctic, yet they remain something of a mystery. The global distribution of seaweeds has not been comprehensively mapped, the full details of their habitats are unknown, their taxonomic classification is incomplete and their biodiversity is not yet understood.[3] But there are reckoned to be about 10,000 kinds of seaweed in the world, and they are essential to the life of the planet. Although

Victorian botanical picture of seaweeds.

we think the oxygen we breathe comes from land plants, marine algae of all sizes provide some 75 per cent of the planet's oxygen supply through photosynthesis, and absorb a huge amount of atmospheric carbon dioxide.[4] And as noted by Darwin, seaweeds play a foundational role in marine

9

ecosystems, providing food and shelter for many marine organisms and for the people and animals that live on them.

One of nature's curiosities, seaweeds – like mushrooms – are neither plant nor animal. While clearly not animals, seaweeds do not have seeds, fruits or the specialized vascular system of plants. Instead, seaweeds draw in nutrients from the sea directly through their surfaces. Seaweeds are usually divided by colour into three groups: red (about 7,000 species), brown (about 2,000 species) and green (about 1,000 species).[5] Many of these have been eaten and used by peoples around the world, in varied ways in different periods in history. A number are known today by their Japanese names, reflecting the fact that Japan pioneered the commercial growing and promotion of edible seaweeds in the modern era.

Red seaweed, the largest and most varied of the groups, includes some of the best-known edible seaweeds, such as *Porphyra* (nori or laver), of which there are more than sixty kinds, and *Palmaria palmata* (dulse, also known as dillisk). This group also includes *Chondrus crispus* (commonly known as carrageen), *Gigartina* and *Eucheuma*, along with *Gelidium* and *Gracilaria*, all of which have natural gelling properties.

Brown seaweed includes the edible kelp family, which flourishes in cold waters, many of which can be eaten. Favourites include *Laminaria*, known as *kombu* in Japan and *haidai* in China, and *Undaria*, called *wakame* in Japan and *qundai-cai* in China.[6] Green seaweed, the smallest of the groups – prime among them the sea lettuce – is relatively delicate, and is found in calm waters close to the shores of temperate zones.

Some seaweeds are eaten or used only within small geographical areas in highly specialized ways dictated by the constraints of local cuisine and custom; others are consumed and used across the world to an extent that is not widely appreciated.

The Hidden Story of Eating Seaweed

Red and brown seaweeds are the sources of phycocolloids, commercial extracts which disperse when they are added to a liquid or a paste, causing it to thicken, stabilize, emulsify, clarify or gel. These properties make them indispensible to the modern mass-market processed food industry, which is, literally, held together by phycocolloids. The idea of using seaweeds as a source of commercial gelatin is not new – its potential was spotted by Sir Joseph Banks at the beginning of the nineteenth century – but no one then could have imagined the extent to which it is now used.[7]

Although gelling agents can also be made from land plants – notably pectin extracted from fruit and guar gum from beans – seaweed phycocolloids are preferred. This is because, while the structure of land plants is rigid, marine plants are more flexible in order to accommodate the waves and currents of the marine environment, and as a result have a unique cell structure that makes them particularly suitable for extracts.[8]

Phycocolloids are tasteless: their contribution to commercial food products lies in their ability to modify viscosity, texture and appearance. In addition to keeping solids and liquids from separating or disintegrating, phycocolloids are used to create desirable 'mouth feel'. They give density and good 'crumb' texture to commercial breads and cakes, make low-fat foods seem thicker and richer, give 'creaminess' to sauces and salad dressings and increase juiciness in processed meat products. Phycocolloids also enhance the visual appeal of foods, improve storage stability, extend shelf life, make food easier to slice, inhibit browning, can clarify wine and give beer a better head of foam.[9] Sometimes marine phycocolloids are mentioned specifically on labels, for example 'agar' and 'carrageenan', or they may be masked by the catch-all phrase 'stabilizers and emulsifiers', or not mentioned at all.

Depending on the brand, the packs of liverwurst or duck and orange *pâté* from the chiller cabinet; fruity jelly beans; frozen cheesecake; deep-dish pizza; commercial Christmas eggnog; ice creams and puddings; ready-made lasagne; bottled salad dressings and chocolate milk; chilled creamy pasta sauces; cartons of creamy coleslaw and commercial soups; breaded fish fingers and processed burgers; canned ham and luncheon meat; fruit yoghurt and mousses; juicy frankfurters, succulent chicken nuggets; the ubiquitous condiment ketchup and countless more commercially produced foods rely on phycocolloids to the extent that most people eat seaweed in this way without knowing it, several times a day.

'Functional' Food, Dysfunctional Uses and Nutrition

Tasty though these ready-made products may be, the over-consumption of high-fat, nutrient-poor, low-fibre processed food is increasingly seen as one of the prime challenges to good health, and seaweed in phycocolloid form is arguably the world's best – or worst – example of the dysfunctional use of a functional food.

Although the term only came into use in the 1980s, 'functional food' originally reflected the observation made by people around the world in many periods of history – that once past the level of basic nourishment, some foods appeared to have an additional positive effect on health and wellbeing. As the Greek physician Hippocrates put it in the fourth century BC: 'Let food be thy medicine and medicine be thy food.'

Advertisement for 'Maraliment', a revitalizing seaweed-based soup, French, 1920.

Once merely anecdotal, the discovery of vitamins in the early nineteenth century and the subsequent development of scientific nutrition set out the five classes of nutrients – proteins, carbohydrates, fats, minerals and vitamins – along with fibre and water, in terms of which foods could be analysed, and correspondences between particular foods, certain medical conditions and optimal health could be established, or at least suggested. Originally, 'functional foods' referred to foods in their natural state, consumed as part of the normal diet. Subsequently, at least for some people, it has also come to mean enhanced – as in 'vitamin-enriched' – foods, and supplements taken in capsule, liquid, dried or powdered form, in addition to the normal diet. However it is defined, seaweeds have emerged as an ideal functional food, and seaweed 'remedies' are found in all coastal cultures, in all periods of history.

Although the levels vary between species, and within a single type depending on the location where it grows and the season it is collected, and also according to how it is prepared, generally seaweeds are extremely nutrient-rich, having a mineral content ten times greater than that found in land plants.[10] It is claimed that seaweed has ten times more calcium than milk, eight times more iron than red meat, and more protein than eggs, wheat or beans.[11] Equally important, seaweeds are high in non-nutrient phytochemicals known as secondary compounds, which are antioxidant and anticholesterolemic,[12] which epidemiological studies suggest can reduce the risk of coronary heart disease, stroke and cancer.[13] Vitamin A, the B vitamins (B1, B2, B3, B6, B12 and folate) and vitamins C and E are found abundantly in seaweed, as are the minerals iodine, calcium, phosphorous, magnesium, sodium, potassium, iron and chlorine, along with the trace elements or micro-minerals manganese, copper, zinc, selenium, chromium and molybdenum,[14] which perform a variety of important health-maintaining roles including oxygen storage, thyroid hormone generation, enzyme formation, energy production and support of immune and insulin functions.

Seaweeds contain large amounts of vitally important protein, the body's primary building blocks for muscle, skin, hair, bone and much else. Protein from red meat is high in saturated fats, implicated in cardiovascular disease. Protein from poultry and fish also contains fat, although in smaller quantities, but seaweed from protein is fat-free, which is why it is increasingly described as the perfect 'heart-healthy' food. Proteins can also be obtained from land plants such as legumes, soy and beans, but the cultivation of plant proteins puts a heavy burden on the terrestrial environment, and some of them contain high levels of carbohydrates, while the small amount of carbohydrates in seaweeds are not digested by the human body, and so do not add unwanted empty calories.[15] Seaweed is also used in a range of weight-loss products, based on claims that it is a natural appetite suppressant and raises the body's metabolism. Finally, seaweed has a high level of dietary fibre, which aids digestion. Dr John Harvey Kellogg – inventor of the corn flake and originator of many pioneering dietary practices that are mainstream today – served Japanese seaweed at his famed Battle Creek Sanitarium in the late nineteeth century, to promote digestive regularity and internal cleanliness.[16]

Seaweed is a true superfood. However, the nutritional and health benefits of seaweeds do not transfer into the phycocolloids that are used in the mass-market processed food industry. So, ironically, one of the world's healthiest foods is at present – in the West and increasingly elsewhere – used primarily in the mass-market preparation of unhealthy ones.

'Save the Products of the Land.' U.S. Food Administration poster, 1917.

Eating and Cooking with Seaweed

Seaweed can benefit people at all points along the nutritional spectrum, from the undernourished, for whom it can be used to supplement nutrient-poor diets at a low cost, to those who consume too much starchy, fatty and sugary food, and are looking for healthier alternatives. An increase in seaweed consumption would also improve the health of the planet, by relieving pressure on the production of land plants and animals. This idea is not new. In 1917 during the First World War, the United States Food Administration issued a poster urging people to save the products of the land by eating more fish, which fed themselves on seaweed, among other things. More than a century later, with the seas overfished and the land under even greater pressure, the message is more urgent and direct – instead of eating fish, people should eat seaweed.

Certainly, seaweed is more widely available now than it ever has been. In addition to wild harvesting on the shore

Seaweed farming, using the basic monoline method. The seaweed being grown here is *Eucheuma*, for phycocolloid production.

and from the deep sea, seaweed is being produced around the world using mariculture (growing in the sea) techniques which include the 'monoline method', which involves growing seaweed from nylon lines pegged into the sea bottom; the 'rope method', which uses ropes suspended from floats; and the 'raft' and 'tubular net' methods, which grow seaweed from rafts and floating nets.

The pleasure to be gained by exploring new foods, flavours, textures and cuisines is just as important as health benefits. In many parts of the world, the preoccupation with land-produced food has been so great and long-established that the culinary history and gastronomic possibilities of seaweed are largely unknown. Seaweed is one of the most adaptable of foods. It can be eaten raw on its own, or mixed with many other things. Seaweed can be baked, boiled, simmered, toasted, turned into jelly, fried, smoked, roasted, powdered, pickled, preserved in oil or fermented. It can be ground into meal or flour, chopped and shredded. Seaweed can also be aged or matured to enhance its flavour. It can be distilled into extracts, or made into drinks. The red, brown and green families of seaweed have distinctive culinary flavours – some dried red seaweeds have sulphurous aromas with floral, black-tea notes and a distinctive iodine flavour, while the mild brown seaweeds have different iodine notes, hay-like or spicy aromas and an astringent tang.[17] Some seaweeds are highly flavoured; others are flavourless and take on the taste of whatever they are combined with.

For the most part seaweed is available year-round, although some harvest times are preferred to others. Once harvested and dried, seaweed has a very long storage life, and in this form is light in weight and easy to transport. It reconstitutes readily when put into water, and throughout Asia and elsewhere this has given rise to a distinctive sub-cuisine of soups based on dried prepared and fresh seaweeds. Seaweed is a source of *umami* or glutamate. The so-called 'Fifth Taste', a companion to sweet, salt, bitter and sour, *umami* is often described as the heart and foundation of Japanese cuisine, although it is now recognized and used globally, most recently in what is called the New Nordic Cuisine.[18] While tasteless itself, *umami* – a Japanese word that translates as 'deliciousness' – makes food taste savoury, satisfying, 'meaty' and enjoyable.

Generally, the world at present can be divided between the seaweed eaters of the East and the non-seaweed eaters of the West for whom seaweed is a novelty, a new discovery they associate only with Asian foodways. If you ask most people in Europe and North America if they would eat seaweed, the answer is usually a variation of, 'No, certainly not, why would I eat such a thing?': 'It's just an inedible weed, rubbish on the beach,' 'maybe poor people eat it, during famines,' 'maybe they ate it during wartime, with the food shortages, but no one would eat it willingly.' 'Seaweed is a marginal thing, it has never been important,' 'Maybe people on the other side of the world eat it, but we don't eat seaweed and never have.'

As the following chapters show, seaweed has played a key role in the development of humankind from earliest times in the West as well as in the East, and today the global history and cuisine of seaweed await exploration. By turning from the land to the sea – and thinking 'Blue' instead of 'Green' – there is much to learn and to enjoy.

I

The Beginnings:
Hiding in Plain Sight

As a form of life that goes back at least 500 million years, seaweed is much older than humankind and definitely one of our oldest foods, and yet it has been invisible in the 'official version' of human origins and early diet until very recently, hiding in plain sight.[1]

The New Prehistory of Seaweed

It has long been thought that over many centuries, early humans moved across the globe in a series of migrations, traversing plains and mountains, feeding as they went on hunted animals and on gathered wild foods such as seeds, nuts, roots, fruits and berries. These foods came to be seen as the defining diet of these hunter-gatherers, the original 'Paleo Diet' that gave way to early versions of our modern diet when agriculture, husbandry and sedentary life emerged in the later phases of human development.[2] The migrations were assumed to have been entirely via inland routes; the sea was considered an impassable barrier while coasts were seen as marginal and did not figure in the model. Nor did seaweed.

Resource-rich shoreline terrain, ideal for coastal migration.

The New World was believed to have followed this pattern of inland migration, with the first peoples passing over the Bering Land Bridge (Beringia), which connected Asia and North America, before moving down the centre of the American continent, fanning out and settling. The 'First Americans' were considered to be the Clovis people, so-named after their distinctive stone spear- and arrow-head game-hunting tools, which were found at sites in the interior and dated to around 13,500 years before the present.

Then, in the 1970s, at Monte Verde in southern Chile at a site close to the present-day coast, archaeologists discovered settlement remains which included abundant amounts of several kinds of seaweeds along with smaller algae. Some were found in cooking areas, while others were mixed with other plants and had been chewed, suggesting a medicinal use. When dated, these remains turned out to be older than those of the Clovis people, suggesting that 'an early settlement of South America was along the Pacific coast and that seaweeds were important to the diet and health of early humans in the Americas.'³ Since the first discoveries at Monte Verde, evidence has emerged of early seaweed use along the Peruvian coast and elsewhere.

Highly controversial because they challenged entrenched views about early human movement and diet, the findings at Monte Verde led to new theories of Pacific migration, among them the Kelp Highway Hypothesis. This suggested that the edible resources of the rich coastal ecosystems provided by the great kelp forests that stretch across the North Pacific from Japan to Alaska and down the northwest coast of Canada and America to Baja California facilitated the movement of peoples into the New World, and supported them there once they had arrived.[4]

In many places, movement along the coast was often easier and safer than along the inland routes, and the supply of food would have been more dependable. Later, movement could have been by dugout canoes and sewn-plank boats as well as on foot. Instead of only moving over plains and mountains in pursuit of animals and roots, it is now apparent that people were going along the coast, gathering and eating seaweed, molluscs, fish and other foods. There were therefore two kinds of migration, inland and coastal, and two kinds of 'Paleo Diet' – a land diet and a marine version, in which seaweed played a central part.

In hindsight it is easy to see how seaweed was overlooked in early archaeological and evolutionary theory. In addition to the fact that the coast did not figure in the original inland migration model, changing sea levels mean that some coastal sites are now far from the sea, while many others are under water. Unlike animals, plants, shellfish and fish, seaweeds leave few archaeological traces except in places like Monte Verde, where rare soil and climate conditions favoured

Seaweed salad on a scallop shell.

preservation. Now, however, scientific advances – notably in the fields of isotope analysis and molecular archaeology – are examining artefacts such as bones, teeth and food residue discovered in pots, revealing the extent to which people in all periods ate more marine foods than previously suspected. Generally, where there are large deposits of shells from oysters, clams and other molluscs, archaeologists are beginning to look for traces of seaweed use, since the two grow in proximity.

In Japan, on the other side of the Pacific from Monte Verde, residue analysis led to another instance in which seaweed rewrote prehistory. It had long been assumed that pottery was developed in settled farming communities, and had been invented around 6000 BC in ancient Mesopotamia – present-day Iraq – one of the early cradles of agriculture. The earliest known inhabitants of Japan were the still-mysterious Jōmon people, a hunter-gatherer culture that flourished from about 10,000 BC to 300 BC. Japan is at the eastern end of the great northern Pacific Kelp Highway, and the Jōmon people enjoyed rich marine resources. Moving up and down the coasts, they gathered seaweed and other foods and dived for fish and shellfish which they cooked with liquid in clay pots, making the earliest version of the one-pot dish *nabemono*, which is still enjoyed in Japan today thousands of years later.[5]

It was thought that Jōmon ware dated from the late phases of their culture, but when the residue, including seaweed, from these pots was analysed, the Jōmon vessels were revealed to date from some 12,700 years before the present. This discovery caused as much controversy as the Monte Verde findings. Not only did Jōmon ware become the oldest pottery then known, shifting the centre of innovation from Mesopotamia to Asia. The finds also supported the coastal migration theory; showed that the invention and use of pottery did not depend on sedentary life and agriculture; proved that a marine diet could support a population as successfully, and in as good health, as agriculture could; and established that seaweed had been a central part of the Japanese diet from earliest times.

Ultimately, the Monte Verde and Jōmon findings transformed archaeological understanding of the human past and the place of the sea and seaweed in it, beyond the New World and Japan. Continuing discoveries make it apparent that in many places the continents were settled via the coast as well as by the inland route, with seaweed one of the foundational foods of humankind from the earliest periods. There are kelp highways in the south as well as in the north, in the Atlantic as well as the Pacific, and in warmer waters there are other kinds of seaweed that supported life. After the migration period the coastal areas were not marginal regions, but centres of trade and development, for the Atlantic world as well as the

Asia-Pacific.[6] Instead of facing inwards and concentrating only on the land and its products, archaeologists, historians and many others are learning to face outwards, towards the ocean, seeing it not as a barrier but as a highway and a conduit, with seaweed as a keystone food of humankind.

Early Records of Seaweed

There is a large gap in time between the Jōmon and Monte Verde periods, and the first written reference to seaweed, which is found in the *Epic of Gilgamesh*, sometimes called the world's oldest epic. Written in about 2100 BC in Mesopotamia during the Third Dynasty of Ur, it celebrates the exploits of the demigod hero-king Gilgamesh who, having lost his beloved friend Enkidu to death, goes on a quest to discover the secret of immortality, travelling far from inland Mesopotamia. The wise man Utnapishtim told Gilgamesh to dive to the bottom of the sea, where he would find a plant with stinging thorns which had the power to rejuvenate anyone who ate it.

Weighing himself down with stones to reach the seabed more easily, Gilgamesh located the plant and returned to shore where he intended to give it to the old in order to make them young again, and to eat it himself. Before he did so, Gilgamesh stopped to bathe in a pool and the plant was stolen and eaten by a snake. Ever since, snakes have been able to cast off their skins and grow new ones, but because Gilgamesh lost the plant, humans cannot change their skins, and must grow old and die. Here can be glimpsed the magical, rejuvenating powers that seaweeds are widely believed to have. The method of weighing oneself down with stones to reach the seabed has been used until recently by the pearl divers

Neil Dalrymple,
*Gilgamesh and
the Seaweed of
Immortality*,
2006, stoneware
sculpture.

of the Arabian Gulf, where Gilgamesh is said to have searched, but seaweeds do not have thorns and, as so often in old accounts, it is impossible to identify the plant.

Moving towards the West, in the ancient Mediterranean world the best and most beautiful visual records of seaweed came from the Minoan civilization of Bronze Age Crete (2000–1500 BC), in the form of art rather than of text. Going on the evidence of their surviving artwork, the Minoans loved the sea and its denizens, covering vases and vessels with exuberant naturalistic portrayals of fish, shells and shellfish, octopuses, cuttlefish, coral, starfish and sponges surrounded by swirling seaweed. Many different sorts can be identified, large and small, floating free or attached to rocks. The Minoans had a high marine diet, and it is likely, although not yet proven, that seaweed was eaten in some form – just as pickled seaweed salad is eaten in Crete today. If text mirrors art, there should be an extensive Minoan literature that celebrates the sea and seaweed. However, almost nothing is known of the written language of the Minoans because little has survived, and the fragments that have been translated are mainly basic administrative records rather than descriptive narrative or poetry.

Minoan pottery in the Marine style, showing octopus and drifting seaweed, 15th century BC.

Greeks, Romans and the Fear of Seaweed

With the exception of the Minoans, in historic times seaweed has generally not been highly regarded in the West, due in large part to the Greeks and Romans, from whom much of Western culture stems. Although both Greece and Rome lie on the Mediterranean Sea – the Greek philosopher Plato described the Greeks as 'frogs around a pond' – they were predominantly land-oriented societies, mistrustful and suspicious of the ocean. Seaweed in the Mediterranean is not as lush as in the great oceans, and becomes less abundant at the eastern end, farthest from the Atlantic. Nonetheless, there was sufficient seaweed for the Greeks and Romans to dislike and fear it. To them, the sea was a place of no return, and seaweed the very embodiment of marine menace. The Greek sea god Pontus – older than the Olympian deities – was the god of storms, shipwrecks and drowning men. His hair, and that of his sea-goddess wife Thalassa, consisted of seaweeds which ensnared sailors and pulled them down to their deaths. Similarly, the later sea gods Poseidon (Greek) and Neptune (Roman) had ensnaring hair, and the sounds of the sea were thought to be the sighs of those who had died tangled in seaweed. Like the Greeks, the poets of the Roman Republic emphasized the treacherous and fearful aspects of the sea and classical literature abounds with laments for the drowned.[7]

Seductive death was offered by the Nereids, or sea nymphs, wearing seaweed skirts and garlands, who sometimes helped mariners but more often lured them to fatal embraces in underwater caves – an elemental image that is still embedded in the poetic imagination, as seen in these lines by the poet T. S. Eliot, in 'The Love Song of J. Alfred Prufrock':

The ancient god Pontus, with seaweed hair.

> We have lingered in the chambers of the sea
> By sea-girls wreathed with seaweed red and brown
> Till human voices wake us, and we drown.

Washing about in the shallows, seaweed lay in wait to trap the unwary, as in a poem from the Strasbourg papyrus in which a man wronged by a friend hopes that his betrayer will come to grief on the sea and then struggle ashore, too tangled in seaweed to escape enslavement by the wild Thracians of the coast:

> Still with freezing cold; emerging from the froth
> Clung on to by piles of seaweed
> May he lie like a dog face-down on chattering teeth
> Laid low by his feebleness
> Sprawled at the breakers' edge, still licked at by the surf!

For the Greeks, the shore itself was an ill-omened place to be avoided, home to fishermen burnt black by the sun and regarded as barely human, living by the water in huts made of seaweed.[8] Even cast up on the beaches, seaweed was a frightening thing, as in Book IX of Homer's *Iliad*, when a great storm in the night raised wave on wave, heaving up a tangled mass of seaweed that threw the Achaeans into a panic that ended in their rout by the Trojans. The fear of entanglement lent menace to rumours of a great ocean of seaweed beyond the Mediterranean, the Sargasso Sea, the mysterious gyre in the mid-Atlantic, which for centuries was believed to trap ships and sailors. When Christopher Columbus first sailed across the Atlantic to the New World in 1492, the voyage took 35 days, 23 of which were spent in the Sargasso Sea, where, to the alarm of the crews, the ships were surrounded by floating seaweed so thick it resembled meadows.

To the Greeks and Romans, to go upon the sea was to tempt the gods, and should only be done when absolutely necessary. For them, the land was the proper place for humankind, and the thing that distinguished humans from animals was agriculture and husbandry, the taming of nature by culture. What the Greeks and Romans valued above all else were the

The Sargasso Sea, long feared as a graveyard of ships, on a Wills's Cigarettes card, early 20th century.

cultivated and domesticated products of the land – grain, cattle and wine. Wild-gathered food, regarded as a luxury today, was despised as something for impoverished people only, and seaweed was the wildest of the wild, from a land beneath the waves beyond sight and human control. In the satires of Juvenal, ridicule was heaped on 'inspectors of seaweed' – people who spent their time on unimportant things. To the Greeks and Romans, as the Roman poet Virgil wrote, *nihil vilior alga* – nothing is more vile than seaweed.

Early Greek and Roman naturalists and healers were primarily interested in land plants and remedies, although a few recognized that seaweed might have medicinal and other uses and not all early Greek medical texts have come down to us. In his *Natural History*, Pliny the Elder wrote that external applications of seaweed were beneficial for gout and for pain and swelling of the ankles, and the Greek poet Nicander said that seaweed was a cure for snake bites – although details of these treatments have not survived. There are few detailed descriptions of seaweed from that time, Theophrastus being a rare exception. A contemporary of

Aristotle, Theophrastus wrote of the great seaweed forests in the deep Atlantic, giving special mention to the sugar kelp of 'marvellous size' that grew near the Pillars of Hercules (the Straits of Gibraltar). He also described seaweeds similar to those that drift across the Minoan vases: a feathery one like fennel, that grew on oysters; another with hairy leaves; the shaggy 'sea leek' as high as a man's waist; and others that looked like firs, vines and palms.[9] As for uses, he noted that in Crete a dye was made from seaweed that was even more beautiful than the renowned murex purple, but on seaweed as a food Theophrastus was silent. The only time seaweed is mentioned in the writings of Athenaeus, the great chronicler of the foods of antiquity, it is as the sustenance and hiding place of fish, not something for humans to eat themselves.

And so there are no seaweed recipes or detailed remedies from ancient Greece and Rome, only the legacy of disdain for seaweed eating which is part of Western mainstream culture, and the enduring use of seaweed in poetry and art as a symbol of marine death, danger and desolation.

Seaweed in Arabic Medicine and Warfare

From pre-Islamic times, the Arabs were enterprising voyagers and traders, sailing the Arabian Sea and beyond to the Far East, and by the start of the ninth century they dominated the seas from the Indian Ocean to the Atlantic. Arab mariners were encouraged to make detailed observations of waves, currents and marine life and were familiar with many kinds of seaweed, using them as an aid to navigation, recognizing that seaweed could provide information on winds, tides, depth and conditions on the sea bottom. Arab voyagers reported that some peoples seen on their travels fed seaweed

Seaweed as a symbol of marine danger and desolation in Félix
Bracquemond's *La Mer*, late 19th or early 20th century.

to livestock. The Arabs do not appear to have eaten seaweed themselves, although nothing in the Qur'an forbids it, but they used it extensively in medicine. Some Arab physicians were aware of Greek writings on seaweed and freshwater algae, but they developed their own systems and used seaweeds and algae much more extensively than the Greeks ever did, distinguishing many kinds which physicians and chemists prescribed to reduce pain and fever and to treat cirrhosis, cancer, kidney ailments, enlarged spleens, jaundice, arthritis, haemorrhoids, skin diseases and blood clots, among other conditions.[10] The Arabs were familiar with agar, and unlike the Greeks they gave detailed instructions for its preparation, which involved boiling and drying it and then mixing it with oil. Agar oil was used to treat arthritis, rheumatism, skin ailments and muscular spasms, and when blended with the juice of unripe grapes it was used to treat constipation and diseases of the eye, ear, nose and throat.

The most dramatic use of seaweed by the Arabs came in warfare. During the battles between the Greeks and Arabs for control of the eastern Mediterranean in the seventh century, the Greeks used the notorious 'Greek fire' – an incendiary

'Greek fire' in use, as depicted in an illuminated manuscript, the *Madrid Skylitzes*, 12th century.

liquid sprayed on or at enemy ships, which burned fiercely even on water – enabling the Greeks to destroy the Arab military fleets. Tradition states that Abd al-Rahman, the master of the Alexandria shipyards, devised a method of fire protection which involved coating the ships with an algin extract from *Cystoseira barbata* – a brown seaweed that grows profusely along the Alexandrian coast. Alginates have natural fireproofing qualities, and the coating saved the Arab ships from destruction by Greek fire.[11] Even today, fibres treated with alginate are used in protective clothing for firemen.

Seaweed and Thalassotherapy

Ironically, many centuries after the ancient Greeks and Romans disdained it, a therapeutic use of seaweed was invented and promoted in their name. Bathing in fresh or mineral water as an aid to health and beauty reached elaborate heights under the Romans. Seawater did not enjoy the same popularity, because it was considered corrosive, useful only as a therapy for leprosy and for skin conditions such as ulcers, eczema and unhealed wounds and sores. It is thought that in the first century AD the Roman emperor Tiberius suffered from a disfiguring skin condition that caused him to withdraw to the island of Capri in order to bathe regularly in the sea there at a beach below his cliff-top villa – still known as the Bagni di Tiberio, or Bath of Tiberius – which boasts high salt levels, refreshingly cool water and natural currents that act like massaging water jets.

The therapeutic use of sea-bathing was revived in Europe in the eighteenth century, when a decline in health connected to urbanization and industrial pollution made visits to the seashore fashionable. The wildness that had once been despised was now valued for its vigour and purity, with marine substances – including seaweed – seen as the very opposite of the polluted products of industry. There was a craze for therapeutic sea bathing led in England by Dr Richard Russell, the inventor of the Brighton seawater cure, whose motto, borrowed from Euripides, was 'The sea washes all mankind's evil away'. Russell claimed that

> the vast collection of waters which we call the sea . . . frequently washes whatever is contained between its opposite shores such as submarine plants, salts, fishes, minerals etc, and is enriched with the particles it receives from these bodies . . . they act more powerfully by getting in at the pores of the skin than if the same had been taken by mouth.[12]

The theory behind the treatments was that the skin is the body's largest organ, giving a maximum surface area through which the vitamins, minerals and amino acids in seaweeds can be absorbed. This is how seaweed itself takes in nutrients from the sea and although there is no proof that it works in the same way in the human body, enthusiasts believe it does. Furthermore, they see it as a form of eating – thus the use of the term 'skin food'.

In order to inspire confidence in sea cures, promoters touted them as 'the Healing Arts of the Ancients'. References were made to the healers of classical antiquity, such as Galen and Hippocrates, and the cures began to be called 'thalassotherapy', using the Greek word for the sea, *thalassa*, ignorant of the terrifying aspects of the ancient sea goddess of the same name. Patients on the Brighton cure had their skin rubbed with fresh seaweed and across the Channel on the Atlantic coast of France, things were taken even further.

Paul Gauguin, *The Seaweed Gatherers*, 1888.

The seaboard province of Brittany has poor soil but is rich in seaweed, lying next to a kelp forest which stretches from Norway to Portugal. The *Laminaria* (kelp), a brown seaweed that piles up on the beaches of Brittany, had long been used as fertilizer to enrich the land, and many other seaweeds, called *goémon* locally, grow along the coast. The harvesting of *goémon*, with the wild sea and rugged coast as background, was a favourite subject for artists such as Paul Gauguin and Alfred Guillou. Brittany was known for its shellfish and fish, and the locals had long made a speciality which is still sold there today – *beurre des algues* or minced seaweed in butter – which is used to cook fish or is spread on bread to accompany oysters, scallops and crustaceans. But these culinary pleasures were not of interest to the spa builders. Reasoning that a direct application of sea plants to the body would be

Alfred Guillou,
Seaweed Picker,
1899.

beneficial, French sea-cure promoters developed treatments in which the benefits of seawater were mixed with those of seaweed. Spas in Brittany offered regimes of hot, cold and warm seaweed baths, seaweed vapours, seaweed body packs, wraps and seaweed rubs that were described as 'palliative', 'revitalizing' and 'restorative' for rheumatism, arthritis and skin complaints.

Clients were immersed in murky baths, massaged with exfoliating ointments and wrapped in oozing marine mud, all containing seaweed and smelling of the ocean. Later these claims about the benefits of seaweed treatments were expanded to include the reduction of premature ageing and symptoms of menopause, the establishment of cellulite

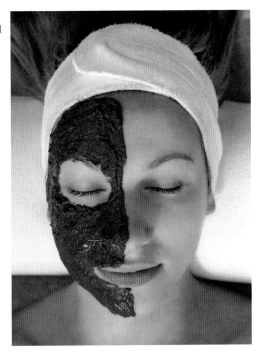

Feeding the skin
– a seaweed facial
mask.

control and weight loss, the diminishing of fatigue and back pain, and the alleviation of depression and other stress-related conditions. The thalassotherapy that originated in Brittany is now practised around the world, using fresh or processed seaweed.

From health, it was a short step to beauty, with seaweed facials and seaweed creams which claimed to preserve a youthful appearance and keep the complexion clear and fresh by improving circulation and tightening the skin. This was the beginning of the modern seaweed cosmetics industry, in which claims about ancient beauty secrets – Cleopatra was often invoked although there is no evidence that she used seaweed cosmetic treatments – have given way to 'scientific' claims about oxygenation, hydration, pH balance and detoxification. It is asserted that different seaweeds have different beauty benefits when applied externally – kombu (kelp) is deemed to have anti-ageing properties; Irish moss or carrageen, *Chondrus crispus*, is said to be especially good for hydration; and bladderwrack for purifying and stimulating lymphatic drainage.[13] Seaweed therapies can be enjoyed at spas, or at home using the many seaweed creams, baths, gels and scrubs on sale at pharmacies, drugstores, cosmetic counters, beauty bars and health food shops. Do-it-yourself treatments can also be made, using commercial, dried seaweed mixed with water, sea salt and vitamin and aromatic oils. Dark and intense aromatics distilled from bladderwrack and carrageen are used in the blending of fine perfumes. Unlike the seaweed phycocolloids in processed foods, the seaweed extracts in marine beauty and body preparations are actively promoted and find a ready market in the West among people who believe in seaweed's beauty benefits – but who would not think of eating it.

Thalassotherapy notwithstanding – as Homer wrote, man is the vainest of all creatures – it is easy to see how seaweed eating became culturally invisible in the West. Coastal migration studies of Europe are in their infancy; most European societies were agricultural and pastoral rather than coastal, and the Graeco-Roman cultural disdain for seaweed was pervasive and persuasive even today, when efforts are being made to rebrand seaweed as 'sea vegetables' in order to escape the ancient disapproval. However, seaweed-eating did exist in Europe in the past, and still does today, revitalized by influences from Asia where seaweed has always been eaten, as will be seen in the next chapters.

2

Seaweed in Japan

Comprised of 6,852 islands in the northeastern Pacific Ocean, Japan has relatively little land that is suitable for crops and pasture, but the scarcity of land resources is made up for by the bounty of the sea. Two great ocean currents wrap around the long, narrow Japanese island chain – the warm Japan, or Black, Current and the cold Okhotsk Current – creating a variety of nutrient-rich marine ecosystems from the subarctic to the subtropical, where fish, shellfish and seaweeds flourish.[1] There are some 2,000 kinds of seaweeds in Japanese waters, many of which are edible and at the heart of what the Japanese call *wa-shoku* – 'our way of eating'. Traditionally, the Japanese ate seaweed every day, often at every meal. The best-known and most widely eaten seaweeds in Japan are wakame, nori and kombu (kelp).

Kombu (Kelp)

The northernmost main island of Hokkaido lies on the Great Kelp Highway, and kelp has been harvested there since pre-historic times. Although kelp grows in cold waters around the world, many connoisseurs believe that Hokkaido kelp is

Kubo Shunman (1757–1820), *Cakes and Food Made of Seaweed.*

the best for flavour, texture and nutritional content. A giant seaweed that can grow many metres in length, there are several species of kombu, each with distinctive shapes, flavours and other qualities. Over 95 per cent of Japan's kombu still comes from Hokkaido, made into stock (*dashi*) or eaten as a main ingredient. It was kelp residue that was found in ancient Jōmon cooking pots from Hokkaido, which is home to the Ainu, one of Japan's indigenous peoples, now thought by many to be descended from the Jōmon.[2]

Like the Jōmon, the traditional Ainu way of life involved hunter-gathering rather than agriculture, and seaweed – especially kelp or kombu – was a staple of their diet, along with fish and shellfish. A remarkable handscroll by Hirasawa Byozan (1822–1876), now in the British Museum, depicts seaweed harvesting among the Ainu of Ezo. The scroll shows Ainu people 'fishing' for kombu from small boats, dredging it from the bottom with long-handled hooks, scythes and rakes, then chopping it up on the beach to make their famed savoury *ohaw* soup, a kelp broth with additions of fish, shellfish and game. Fresh kombu was spread out on the beach to dry, then tied into great bundles which were carried on bent backs to the places where visiting merchants from the southern islands weighed, sorted, graded and bought the seaweed. The scroll also shows the Ainu gathering *tengusa*, used to make agar, and *funori*, similar to carrageen, which they carried from the beach in large baskets, spread out on frame platforms to dry in rough sheets and then rolled up in large bamboo mats for transport and storage.

Ainu eating their famed *ohaw* seaweed soup, late 19th century.

By the early medieval period, from which the first Japanese written records date, the Ainu were already being treated as subject peoples by the Japanese of the southern islands, who obliged them to send regular tributes of choice kelp to the royal court at Nara and then at Heian-kyō, modern Kyoto.

The Ainu were not the only people to be taxed. The Taihō Code, an early administrative and legal code enacted in AD 703, specified that all adult Japanese males in the provinces had to pay tax to the central government in valuable local products, such as silk and silk floss, dyes, lacquer and the best-quality seaweeds, which were sent to the royal court.[3] The elite also had fine seaweeds sent from the coast to their mansions in the capital.

The Heian period (AD 794–1185) was when many features of Japanese culture emerged, including Japan's distinctive cuisine in which food prepared in an elaborate manner was arranged decoratively on carefully chosen serving ware. There were not yet any samurai and, as this was a time of peace, culture rather than military prowess became the arena in which courtiers sought to distinguish themselves. Poetry, the arts, specialized knowledge, sartorial style and material display flourished at court, turning the period into a golden age of taste and refinement. The earliest Japanese poems referring to seaweed were written during the Nara and Heian periods, such as this one from the collection of ancient poetry known as the *Manyōshū* compiled around AD 759, in which the movements of a girl are likened to those of the seaweeds she collects:[4]

> To my memory comes spontaneously the beautiful girl
>   Tekona
> Who will have cut and reaped the fine seaweed,
> Bending and yielding (with the waves)
> In the Bay of Mama in Katsushika.[5]

The grace of the girls who gathered seaweed was a recurrent theme in early Japanese seaweed poetry, along with imagery of love and longing:

> So she who lay with me
> As yielding as the seaweed to the wave,
> Passed and was gone,
> As leaves of autumn pass and are no more.[6]

Love and longing are mixed with smoke from seaweed burning on a beach, in this poem by the Heian poet Fujiwara no Hideyoshi (1184–1240):

> From huts on the shore
> Where sea folk burn the briny wrack
> Smoke rises in the dusk,
> As rumour rises to my hurt
> From these still smouldering fires of love.[7]

Seaweed gathering and salt-making were linked activities. *Moshiogusa* was seaweed on which brine was repeatedly poured and allowed to dry until it was thoroughly permeated with salt. The briny seaweed ('briny wrack') was then burned and the residue was put into water where the salt dissolved and was separated from the ashes. This concentrated brine was then evaporated, leaving behind the pure salt.[8]

Another poem expressed sentiments familiar to all lovers of seaweed:

> Shall I not miss the dainty seaweed
> On the rugged island beach
> When it is hidden under the flood tide?[9]

Katsushika Hokusai (1760–1849), *Gathering Seaweed.*

These poems do not refer to the rugged Ainu and the robust kelp of the deep north. Seaweeds were gathered all around the coasts of Japan, with different sorts flourishing in different locations. A landscape of connoisseurship developed, with the seaweeds of certain areas acknowledged to be the best of their kinds. In the early medieval period, wild-gathered seaweed was a great luxury, rarely eaten by the common people and generally reserved for the elite. Newly translated records describe the guests of Prince Nagaya (684–729), grandson of Emperor Tenmu, feasting in 'a garden where cranes danced', drinking sake over ice that had been brought from a special ice house and gazing at the stars while dining on delicacies such as choice seaweed sent to the Prince from Shima province.[10]

Seaweed was also essential for rituals. Japanese culture is known for its sensitivity to the seasons and harmony with nature, which is rooted in the ancient religion of Japan, the animistic worship of *kami* – nature spirits, elemental forces, the spirits of place, local and regional deities, and the gods and goddesses of sun, moon and storm. A figure of some 3,000 *kami* has been given, but they were countless. Out of this grew what became the state religion, known as Shinto today. Even after the introduction of Buddhism, the old religion remained, and remains, at the heart of Japan's culture and culinary practice.[11] In order to keep chaos and misfortune at bay and to ensure the fertility of the land, sea and people, the emperor and the court had to perform a perpetual series of rituals in which the key foods of life were offered to the gods, including rice, sake, abalone, fresh, dried and pickled fish, and – always – several kinds of seaweed. These were presented to the gods with elaborate ceremony, while the priests recited prayers like this:

> The fruits of the mountain fields
> The sweet herbs and the bitter herbs
> As well as the fruits of the blue ocean
> The wide-finned and the narrow-finned fishes
> The sea-weeds of the deep and the sea-weeds of the
> shore,
> All these various offerings do I place, raising them high
> Like a mountain range, and present.[12]

More than 1,000 years later, the same sacred foods are offered at Shinto shrines today.

At the Heian court, much attention was paid to the ceremony, etiquette and presentation of food, but for all its elegance, the elite Heian diet was nutritionally poor, and the health of the courtiers was not generally good.[13] Most of the calories came from high-status polished rice, along with other grains and roots like the sweet potato. In the ninth century, under the influence of Buddhism, Emperor Saga (r. 809–823) forbade the eating of all meat except that of fish, shellfish, crustaceans and birds, a prohibition that remained in force until the nineteenth century. Vegetables were usually eaten cooked or pickled, rather than fresh and raw. Fish, the main protein source, were often dried, smoked or salted. The cookery techniques were based on fire and water – boiling, steaming, simmering and grilling. Oil and frying were not used because oil was not plentiful and in any case, was regarded as ritually impure, with the result that the diet lacked sufficient fat. In this restricted diet, seaweed played a key role in providing much-needed minerals, especially iodine, and it formed the basis of the monastery soups that sustained the growing communities of purely vegetarian Buddhist monks.

Under the Kamakura, Muromachi and Ashikaga Shogunates which followed the Heian era, power shifted from the emperor to military leaders supported by the new warrior caste of samurai, which in turn gave rise to a merchant class that catered to their needs. The spread of Buddhism led to an increase in seaweed consumption, and during periods of warfare seaweed which could be dried, stored and easily transported was an ideal food for warriors as well as those who were being besieged. Trade now supplemented tribute, and from the fourteenth century Japanese merchants travelled regularly to Hokkaido to obtain supplies of kombu from the Ainu.

Fleets of merchant ships carried the dried kombu south from Hokkaido to ports along the Sea of Japan, and after landing it was transported inland and traded abroad as far as China via the Ryukyu Islands.[14] Different regions and cities along the trade route developed their own ways of using kombu, contributing to Japan's varied seaweed cuisine, which was no longer restricted only to the elite.

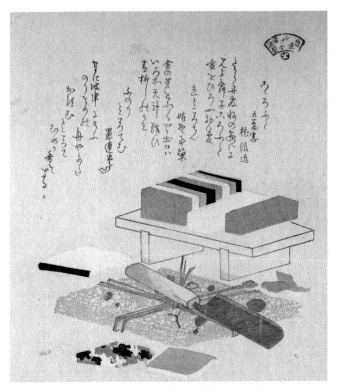

Kubo Shunman (1757–1820), *Seaweed Food and Kitchen Utensils.*

In Toyama on the Sea of Japan, marinated sashimi (raw fish) was wrapped in kombu, as was *kamaboko* (fish cake). Called *kombu maki*, these kelp wraps became widely popular, especially at New Year, when 'lucky' foods are eaten to bring good fortune in the coming year. In Japanese, 'kombu' is a play on the word *yorokubu*, which means happiness, so kelp is considered an auspicious food at any time, but especially at the start of a new annual cycle. The Ainu did not use soy sauce or spices, but as kombu moved south it took on the characteristic flavourings of the Japanese heartland, notably

A dish of kombu simmered with pumpkin.

soy sauce, early versions of which were introduced by Buddhist monks from China in the sixth century.

As the culinary repertoire developed, so did kombu connoisseurship, which continues today, based on type, shape, lustre and even the beach it was harvested from. Light brown in colour, sweet and known as the 'King of Kombu', the wide-leaved Hokkaido *ma-kombu* is the most highly prized, used for making clear stock (*dashi*) or – dried, finely shredded and flavoured with vinegar – sprinkled over rice or soup. Darker in colour and fragrant, *rausu-kombu* is the kelp of choice for *kombu-cha* (kombu tea) and *su-kombu* (pickled kombu), while the more common, thin-leaved *naga-kombu* is considered ideal for *nimono* (simmered vegetable stews).

The city of Osaka became the centre of the kelp trade, giving rise to local specialities such as *oboro* and *tororo kombu* (shaved and shredded kelp) and *kombu no tsukudani* or *shiokombu*, kelp simmered in soy sauce and mirin (sweet rice wine) traditionally eaten as a relish to enliven plain white rice. This was a thrifty dish, because it was made with the kelp that had been used to make *dashi*.

If Japanese cuisine can be thought of as a body, *dashi* is its blood – it is the broth that is the basis of Japanese cookery, commonly made from a combination of kombu and *katsuo-bushi* (dried bonito) but also occasionally shiitake mushrooms and small dried fish. This stock is ubiquitous, used in everything from the most refined *kaiseki* ceremonial dishes to the hearty *chankonabe* stew eaten by sumo wrestlers.[15] The art of *dashi*-making does not involve long boiling, which accentuates the fishy flavours. Instead, the ingredients are only soaked in water and heated briefly, so as to extract the essence without overcooking, and the stock is then strained. As primary (*ichiban*) or secondary (*niban*) *dashi*, it permeates other foods without overwhelming them, heightening their taste through the magic of *umami*.[16]

Dried kombu, *katsuoboshi* (dried bonito) and *niboshi* (dried small fish), the basis of Japan's famed *umami*-rich *dashi* stock.

Umami seibun, the 'tastiness component' as it is known in Japan or the Fifth Taste as it is called in the West, is created by the chemicals monosodium glutamate, sodium inosinate and sodium guanylate.[17] Effective individually, when they are combined they have a synergistic effect on each other, coming together to act as a strong natural flavour enhancer. Monosodium glutamate is present in a number of foods but especially in kombu, so when the kelp is combined with dried fish, a rich source of sodium inosinate, the result is an *umami*-rich *dashi* broth that intensifies the flavour of the foods that are cooked in it, also conveying a sense of freshness and of satisfaction or fullness through a gastronomic alchemy that is not completely understood but is now recognized and valued worldwide.[18]

At the opposite end of the Japanese archipelago from Hokkaido are the southern islands of Okinawa, whose people – like the Ainu – are considered 'not quite Japanese' by the Japanese, having been influenced by China and South Asia through centuries of trade, as reflected in their cuisine in which pork is the favoured meat. The Okinawans are the world's longest-lived population, their longevity attributed to a diet in which seaweed plays a key part.[19] More kombu is eaten in Okinawa than anywhere else on earth. An Okinawa speciality is *tebichi* – sometimes called 'longevity soup' – which is made with seaweed and pork that has had the fat cooked out of it. The soup is rich in collagen as well as in *umami*, and is sometimes combined with soba or buckwheat noodles.

Wakame and Other Seaweeds

By the seventeenth century, an elaborate and sophisticated seaweed cuisine had developed. Written about 1640, the

Kan'ei Cookbook mentioned 21 seaweeds in common use and a variety of techniques for preparing them, including baking, toasting, pan-frying, vinegaring, using in soup and preparing raw in salads.[20] Prime among them was wakame (*Undaria pinnatifida*), an indispensable part of the traditional Japanese diet. With a sweet taste and soft texture that make it extremely pleasant to eat, wakame is the seaweed usually encountered in miso soup.

Growing all along the Japanese coast except for parts of Hokkaido, wakame used to be wild-harvested by fishermen working from small boats using long-handled scythes, but is now grown commercially, although the wild seaweed is preferred because it retains its crispness better. Wakame gathered in the spring can be rinsed, chopped and made into a fresh salad (*sunomono*) lightly dressed with vinegar, or used as a garnish. Wakame can also be vacuum-packed, but it is mainly dried and processed in different ways; one highly prized type – *naruto-wakame* – is treated with ash first, which helps it to keep its colour and aids preservation. Wakame is a favoured ingredient in traditional *aemono*, a salad that is one of the basic categories of Japanese cuisine, consisting of lightly cooked vegetables such as spinach, carrot, bamboo shoots, aubergine, lotus root, string beans and shredded seaweed, in a dressing of soy, sugar and sesame seeds.[21]

Other seaweeds that are widely eaten in Japan and also exported include arame (*Eisenia bicyclis*) and hijiki (*Sargassum fusiforme*), both of which are dark in appearance – brown or black – and are sold dried and usually shredded. They can be boiled, steamed or sautéed, and are cooked with vegetables or with fish, or used cold in salads, as a garnish or mixed with rice. Other seaweeds that are little known in the West because they are not exported are *kajime*, a brown seaweed which is mucilaginous like okra and is made into a cold soup that has

Wakame in light miso soup, a Japanese staple.

been renowned since the medieval period. Another seaweed, *tengusa tokoroten-so*, a red seaweed, is not eaten in its natural form but is boiled down to produce a very firm gelling agent. The finest quality is used for the thick jellies called *yōkan*, which are made with sweetened bean paste, and *kanten*, clear jellies that are often fruit flavoured. Both are firm enough to be sliced into pieces and picked up with chopsticks, and are much chewier than Western gelatin desserts – something Westerners accustomed to wobbly jellies find disconcerting. Related seaweeds are used to make agar, which has a less firm hold and is exported. Seaweed-based gelatins are fibre-rich and suitable for vegetarian and vegan diets.

Many seaweeds are relished as local specialities and have been the object of culinary tourism for centuries, with people travelling far to eat them where they grow and to enjoy the picturesque spectacle of harvesting. For centuries, in an early example of *terroir* marketing, seaweeds were branded by their places of origin and sold widely as choice provincial products, sought out by gourmets and celebrated by artists, as seen in the many *ukiyo-e* prints which show seaweed gathering. Packages of gourmet seaweed inscribed with their places of origin are still a favourite present, called *omiyage*, in Japan's elaborate gift-exchange customs.

Suizen temple in Higo province was famous for its fragrant seaweed soup, and a poem by the seventeenth-century poet Bashō captures the pleasure of a man who is so delighted with it that he gulps down several servings:

A clear soup
is so delicious!
Suizen temple.
At one sitting
eaten!
Food for two days.[22]

Chestnut *yōkan*, firm seaweed gelatin made with red bean paste and chestnut pieces.

So important was seaweed for both local consumption and trade that there were temples and shrines devoted to seaweed all along the coasts of Japan, with Shinto rituals and festivals that were intended to honour the seaweed and ask the gods for continued good harvests. One example of many still observed is the ritual held at the Mekari Shrine overlooking Hayatomo Sound, Fukuoka Province, on the first day of the New Year. Well before dawn, when it is still dark, the priest goes out in the icy waters to cut seaweed at low water, having to keep ahead of the fast-running tides and currents with only a large torch for light. The newly gathered seaweed – the first of the year – is then laid on the altar as an offering, and the ritual is believed to bring good fortune for the coming annual cycle. In the past, the Hayatomo ceremony was held in secrecy and it was forbidden to watch it, but it can now be viewed from a respectful distance by anyone hardy enough to make the trip. The seaweed harvested in this ritual is wakame.

Utagawa Kuniyoshi (1797–1861), *Seaweed Gatherers at Omari*.

Toyota Hokkei, *Seaweed-gathering Ritual of Hayatomo*, early 1830s. A priest is dashing through the waves with a torch and seaweed.

Nori and Sushi

The Japanese seaweed best known and most widely eaten in the West is nori (*Porphyra*). Flourishing in temperate waters, this delicious red seaweed was highly esteemed from ancient times and, as a highly valued wild-gathered product, was specified on the earliest tax and tribute lists. Nori is associated with one of the iconic figures in Japanese history, the first Tokugawa Shogun, Ieyasu (1543–1616). According to tradition,

Ieyasu was very fond of fresh fish and nori. The Shogun commanded local fishermen to bring fish to him daily at his new capital of Edo, later Tokyo. To ensure a constant supply, fishermen built fish-holding pens with bamboo fences in the waters of what is now called Tokyo Bay.

The discovery that nori seaweed grew on the bamboo fences led the Shogun to order that commercial cultivation should be attempted. Initially the procedure was to sink bunches of twigs in tidal waters and to collect the seaweed that grew on them. For the first time, nori was produced in sufficient quantities to be consumed by a wider sector of the population, greatly increasing the desire and demand for it. However, although other kinds of seaweed responded well to cultivation, nori proved difficult to grow dependably for reasons that could not be understood at the time. Good nori harvests were unpredictable and seemed to be a matter of luck, so although it had become more affordable, nori remained a luxury.

As Osaka was the city of kelp, Edo (now Tokyo), near the natural gathering grounds, became the city of nori. Originally nori was dried in its natural state like other seaweeds and eaten toasted and in soups, or boiled and made into paste, like the *tsukudani* made with kombu. During the Edo period (1603– 1868) the seaweed producers of Asakusa, now a part of greater Tokyo, used the basic techniques of papermaking to develop a method of boiling, shredding and then drying seaweed on frames to make into the dried paper-like rectangles of nori which became renowned as a regional food speciality of Edo. The standard size of a sheet of nori is 22.5 × 17.5 cm (9 × 7 in.), sold ten sheets to a bundle.[23]

This is the nori that was used for what is now known around the world as sushi, but was originally called *norimaki* or *makisushi*. Sushi is not an ancient food, having only been

The preparation of *Porphyra*. From a Japanese print.

Preparation of nori sheets in a Japanese print, *c.* 1900.

invented after nori was first made into sheets. Dried in fronds or boiled as a paste, nori had always been eaten with rice. The invention of nori sheets soon led to the development of various forms of nori-wrapped food, beginning in the late eighteenth or early nineteenth century.[24] The simplest method was to place a suitably sized piece of nori, sometimes first dipped in soy sauce, on top of a bowl of rice, and then use chopsticks to enclose some rice in the nori before bringing the morsel to the mouth. This is still common practice when eating at home. Another simple version was the *musube* or rice ball, which involved taking a piquant pickled plum (*umeboshi*), enclosing it in a ball of cooked rice and wrapping the ball in nori.

It was soon realized that more elaborate nori wraps would be perfect for the snacks that were a central part of the culinary life of Japan's bustling capital. *Norimaki* and *makisushi* were tubular rolls of rice with a savoury filling, wrapped in nori with the aid of a *makisu* mat and cut into slices so that the colours of the filling would contrast with the whiteness of the rice and the darkness of the nori. Traditional favourites include *kappa maki*, the cucumber-filled roll, named in honour of the kappa or green frog-like water spirit; *shinko-maki*, filled with yellow pickled daikon or *takuan* (radish); and *tekka-maki*, commonly made with raw tuna. These fillings became more elaborate over time, and different styles of slicing developed: thin, medium and thick. There is now the *uramaki* style, which is a seaweed roll with the nori on the inside, giving a pinwheel effect, and the *temaki* style, consisting of rice and fillings in a hand-rolled cone.

Nori sheets soon began to be used on *nigirisushi*, also called *edomaesushi* because it originated in Edo. From the early nineteenth century, these snacks consisted of a small piece of shaped, cooked rice topped with raw or cooked fish, shell-fish or other ingredients, and these sometimes incorporated nori, most commonly when strips of nori were used to hold the sushi ingredients together and give a pleasing contrast of

Musube rice balls wrapped in nori.

Various types of *makisushi* and *nigirisushi* in the Edo style.

colour and texture. There are local and regional varieties of *makisushi* and *nigirisushi* but the Edo style has become dominant. Although sushi is ubiquitous today, this was not always so.

As noted above, although systematic seaweed farming was underway in Japan by the seventeenth century, nori did not respond well to cultivation, so it remained in relatively short supply. No one could understand why nori was so difficult to grow compared to other types of seaweed. This continued until the 1930s, when Dr Kathleen Drew-Baker, a British scientist studying *Porphyra* using specimens gathered in Wales, finally unravelled its complex reproductive cycle. No one in Britain was interested in her discovery, and then the Second World War broke out. After the war was over, Drew-Baker contacted colleagues in Japan who immediately realized that her discovery would make commercial cultivation of nori possible for the first time. The Japanese post-war economy was in ruins and the national health at a low ebb after years of privation, so commercial production of nori for domestic consumption and for export would be a double boon. Thanks to Drew-Baker's discovery and subsequent

Mother of the Sea Dr Kathleen Drew-Baker.

work by Japanese scientists and cultivators, modern seaweed mariculture was born, nori became widely available in Japan for the first time and sushi became a popular everyday snack. Although she never visited Japan herself, every year Drew-Baker is honoured as 'the Mother of the Sea' in a ceremony at a shrine on Ariake Bay in Kumamoto Prefecture overlooking a prime nori-producing area. The ritual commemorates her contribution to the Japanese seaweed industry, to the Sushi Revolution, and to nori.

After the Second World War, a number of factors came together to make sushi a world food. First, there was curiosity in the West about Japanese culture, including a cuisine that was visually splendid but also seemed very strange – one early American report described sushi as 'rice sandwiches'.[25] The 1960s vogue for Zen, macrobiotic eating and vegetarianism increased interest in nori and seaweed in the West, and with the economic boom of the 1970s, called the 'Japanese economic miracle', all things Japanese became fashionable and sushi went mainstream and global.[26] In the climate of the time, the papery black substance that sushi was wrapped in seemed like another ingenious Japanese invention – an edible paper. The fact that it was seaweed did not register with everyone. California, the American state where hippie and yuppie met, was the sushi beachhead, the place where one of the first fusion versions was invented – the California roll, made with nori, rice and avocado, to which crabmeat and cucumber were sometimes added. Young people of Generation X – the American cohort born between 1961 and 1981 – were called 'Generation Sushi' because they took it up with

California roll sushi of crab, avocado and cucumber wrapped in nori, with the rice around the outside, in the *uramaki* style.

such enthusiasm, and soon sushi was to be found in cities internationally.

A generation on from the Sushi Revolution, global sushi is developing its own sub-cuisines. The largest populations of ethnic Japanese outside Japan live in Brazil and Peru, the result of immigration to work on plantations there in the nineteenth century. Over time, this has given rise to sushi that mixes tropical flavours and foods with Japanese culinary sophistication and their passion for the freshest ingredients. Peruvian-Japanese (*Nikkei*) cuisine is known for sushi that uses the superb fish, seaweed and seafood of the Pacific coast – sushi stuffed with ceviche, with shrimp and palm heart, or with crab, avocado and pepino, a fruit that is like a melon crossed with a pear. These might be served alongside Peruvian salads, which combine ingredients like seaweed, edamame beans, corn, tomato, onions and coriander (cilantro), with a dressing of oil, rice vinegar and *togarishi*, Japanese chilli salt. Brazilian-Japanese sushi is more flamboyant – mango and kiwi are favoured fillings, as is cream cheese, and deep-frying is popular. Nori-wrapped sushi filled with salmon and cream cheese or other morsels is battered and deep fried, often served drizzled with chilli mayonnaise or tropical fruit sauces garnished with limes and fresh seaweed, while exotic *temaki* – hearty sushi made in a rolled nori cone – is a much-loved street food.

Japan's intensive promotion of Japanese cuisine and seaweed in all its forms accounts for the fact that although Japan is no longer the largest producer of edible seaweed, its products are a byword for quality, and many seaweeds and foods made from them are known around the world by their Japanese names.

3
Seaweed in China and Korea

Like Japan, China has a long history of seaweed use, but with a slightly different emphasis. While the Japanese focus has always been primarily on seaweed as food, in China seaweed was originally thought of and treated as medicine.

Traditional Chinese medicine is based on a complex system of balances and correspondences attributed to the mythic Yellow Emperor, said to have reigned from 2696 to 2597 BC. 'His' *Huangdi Neijing* (Classic of Internal Medicine) was only compiled in around 200 BC, but it contains material that was handed down orally from much earlier periods. Part philosophy and part medical text, the *Huangdi Neijing* has changed over the centuries, but certain elements remain standard, with the basic principles as follows. The universe is composed of energy (*ch'i*) expressed in the dual powers Yin (female/moon/light) and Yang (male/sun/darkness), which are in turn embodied in, among other things, five elements (metal, water, wood, fire and earth), five seasons (spring, summer, late summer, autumn and winter), five colours (green, red, yellow, white and black), five climates (wind, heat, humid, dry and cold), five viscera (liver, heart, spleen, lungs and kidneys), five internal systems (gall bladder, small and large intestines, stomach and bladder) and five flavours (sour, bitter, sweet,

Seaweed is used in traditional Chinese medicine, fresh, dried, powdered and made into infusions.

pungent and salt), all of which are linked to each other in different ways.[1]

Ideally, vital energies circulate through the body in dynamic and balanced harmony – this is the 'normal' state of health. Illnesses are caused by interruptions of normal functions, and order and balance are restored through the use of medicines.[2] As the Yellow Emperor put it, 'health means restoration to order.'[3] In the *Huangdi Neijing* the diagnosis and prescription might be as follows: 'When the liver suffers from an acute attack, one should quickly eat sweet food to calm it down' or 'laboured breathing may be treated with prescriptions for "elevating the ch'i".'[4] Medical practitioners then had to turn to the immense pharmacopoeia seen in traditional Chinese medicine shops today – mysterious plants, fungi, animals, fish, shells, birds, reptiles, roots, insects and seaweeds – each embodying the elements in different ways, with ingredients further distinguished by region of origin, season of the year and even time of the day or night they were gathered, and what part of the plant or animal was being used. These are then made up to individual order – ground and swallowed, or left whole and brewed into an infusion for drinking – in order to balance internal energy and restore normal function. The art lies in combination. Chinese medicines use many ingredients in each prescription in order to set up an internal dynamic and generate the right kind of energy for the complaint.

Coming into this complex web of medicinal cures and beliefs, seaweed was considered invigorating and cooling and was associated with yang and with both bitter and salty flavours.[5] Goitre – a disfiguring condition which we now know is caused by iodine deficiency – is described in ancient Chinese texts as resulting from 'hardening' or 'stagnation', and was treated with the 'invigorating' properties of *kun bu* (kombu or *Laminaria* seaweed), which is rich in iodine. Responding to disease that has already manifested is called 'reactive medicine', but in China preventative medicine was and is considered more important, and this is where cookery comes in. The *Huangdi Neijing* advocated healthy everyday eating over reliance on medication: 'From olden times the sages prepared soups, liquids . . . and medicines, but their special emphasis was on the preparation. Thus from olden times these soups and liquid medicines were prepared, but not swallowed as medicines.'[6] Preparation followed the theory of the elements. Each of the five flavours was thought to have an effect on the human body: in the right amounts, salty flavour has a softening effect, but too much of it hardens the pulse; bitter flavours have a strengthening effect, but in excess they wither the skin; correct amounts of sweet flavour have a retarding effect but too much causes aches in the bones; sour flavour has a gathering (stringent) effect but a surplus can toughen the flesh; and pungent flavours have a dispersing effect, but too much can knot the muscles.[7] At some stage, preservation methods such as fermentation and pickling and cookery techniques were incorporated into the scheme – boiling, poaching and steaming are associated with yin; roasting, stir-frying and deep-frying with yang. Traditional Chinese cookery was therefore as much an exercise in preventative medicine as gastronomy, with different combinations of flavours and ingredients cooked in particular ways originally intended to maximize wellness and normal function as well as please the palate. Many early Chinese recipes look more like prescriptions, describing the effects of the ingredients rather than their taste. As Sun Szu-mo, an early (*c.* AD 581–682) medical practitioner put it, 'one should treat illness first with diet. If the patient does not recover, only then should medicine be ordered.'[8] From earliest times, China epitomized the principle of 'food as medicine', in which seaweed played an increasing part.

There are references to seaweed pickled with salt and vinegar in the *Chih Min Yao Shu* manual dating from about AD 544, and to seaweed fermented with soy paste in the *Wu Shih Chung Khuei Lu*, which dates from the late Song Dynasty (*c.* AD 960–1276).[9] In ancient texts published for the use of the elite, references are made to 'seaweed wine', a recipe for which was given in the *Chou Hou Pei Chi Fang* (Prescriptions for Emergencies) dating from about AD 340:

Seaweed Wine

Wash off the salt on one catty of seaweed (*hai tsao, Sargassum siliquastrum*). Place it in a silk bag and soak it in two pints of clear wine (*ching chiu*). In spring or summer, after two days drink two *ko* of the wine at a time until the wine is depleted on the third day. Repeat the soaking in

服藥食忌

Illustration from the dietary manual *Yin-Shan Cheng-Yao*, prepared for the Mongol emperor, Ming period (1368–1644). The doctor here is advising that drugs containing liquorice are incompatible with Chinese cabbage and seaweed.

another two pints of wine. Drink the wine as before. The residue is then dried and also taken internally.[10]

Pleasant to drink, it was also a therapy for goitre. The *Wai Tai Mi Yao* of AD 752 gives recipes for seaweed medicinal pastilles, one involving both *hai tsao* and *hai tshai* or *kun pu* (*Laminaria saccharina*). These were pulverized, mixed with honey to form pills the size of plum stones and then sucked like a boiled sweet or piece of candy.[11]

In the many herbals and commentaries that were used in medical practice, seaweed is very much a rarity compared to land-sourced ingredients. This can be seen in the *Yin-Shan Cheng-Yao*, a dietary manual prepared for the Mongol emperor of China in 1330 intended to safeguard his health. Full of recipes which do not distinguish between food and medicine, it reflects an imperial court amply provided with all the exotic goods that the great Mongol empire could command, except for seaweed, which was clearly scarce and reserved for elite medicinal use. In one passage, the emperor is cautioned not to eat seaweed if he had just taken a medicine containing liquorice.[12] On this occasion, the seaweed was *Sargassum fusiforme* or *S. Paddadum*, often drunk as a medicinal tea, but also taken as pills. More than 500 years after the Mongol emperors, *Sargassum* was one of the ingredients in the 'Pill for Soothing the Liver and Softening Masses' prepared by the imperial physicians for the Emperor Guangxu (1871–1908).[13] Recent studies suggest that 'Sargassum has anti-inflammatory, anticancer, antimicrobial, antivital, liver protective and antioxidant activity.'[14] The *Yin-Shan Cheng-Yao* also advised the Mongol emperor that 'seaweed is salty in flavour and cooling. It is slightly rank and lacks poison. It is good for goiter. It destroys ch'i knots and tumorous swelling. Too much should not be eaten.'[15] In this case the seaweed was *kan bu* or kombu.

Chinese Imperial dragon robe, silk tapestry weave (*kesi*), Qing Dynasty (1780–1850), embroidered with the Twelve Symbols of Sovereignty. The seaweed is usually placed near the bottom, rising from the waves at the hem.

The importance of seaweed is shown by the fact that it was one of the Twelve Symbols of Sovereignty embroidered on the dragon robes worn by the emperors of China since ancient times, representing purity and the element water. The other symbols are sun, moon, stars, mountain, dragon, phoenix, grail or goblet, fire, rice, axe and *fu* (bow).

The Mongol emperor's seaweed came from far away. Although China has a long coastline, its coastal waters are relatively warm and not as conducive to seaweed growth as the seas off Japan. Initially, therefore, supplies were limited and records show that as early as the fifth century AD

China was importing iodine-rich kombu from Hokkaido. Later, other seaweeds were imported from Japan, Korea and Southeast Asia in fleets of junks and traded inland along with seaweeds gathered on China's coast, although it is not always possible to identify species by early descriptions, such as 'uncombed hair'.[16] Over time seaweed imports continued, references to seaweed became more frequent in old Chinese texts and culinary usage developed, as described by a visiting Western naturalist in the 1880s:

> And seaweeds generally are much more in demand for food than formerly . . . we have the edible bird's nest, the yang-tsai, *Laurencia papillosa*; the iced jelly sold in hot weather which is prepared from the tengusa or *Gelidium corneum*; the *Laminaria saccharina*, boiled with the pork and served as a vegetable, the *Chorda filum* that comes to the table with the meat or broth; the *Graciliaria spinosa* that gives the agar agar and forms the bulk of the cargoes of the junks returning from Singapore.[17]

The seaweed *Arachnoidiscus japonicus* was also used by the Chinese, the naturalist noted, for packing porcelain and other articles for export. The Chinese government considered seaweed sufficiently important to include it in the goods they brought to the great International Health Exhibition held in London in 1884, a pioneering event that aimed to promote the preservation of good health through practical and inexpensive ideas that could easily be adapted for everyday life. Exhibitors came from all over the world, and food and natural products for healthy eating and living were a prime focus. The Japanese presented sake wine and tofu to the British public, and the Chinese opened a dining pavilion at the exhibition – the first Chinese restaurant in Britain – which

The Eight Main Methods used to Prepare Seaweed in China

Shao, or 'red cooking', is when the seaweeds are quickly fried and then simmered in water along with soy and other ingredients for thirty minutes to two and a half hours, a method that produces a lot of gravy.

Chao, or stir-frying in a wok, involves frying the seaweed and other ingredients over a high heat in oil that has been flavoured with garlic, onion and ginger.

Ging dun, the clear simmering process, consists of simmering the main ingredient for up to five hours until it becomes tender, after which dried seaweed and other ingredients are added.

Zeng is the process of steaming dried seaweed for 15 to 25 minutes, then cutting it into small pieces and dipping it into condiments. This is reckoned to be one of the best methods of preparing dried seaweed.

Jian involves frying dried seaweeds in shallow oil, then dipping the seaweeds into condiments such as soy sauce, chilli oil, sesame oil or mixtures of these combined with ingredients such as chopped fresh ginger.

Tang (or scalding) is a method in which fresh seaweed is placed in boiling water for a few minutes, drained and cut into pieces before condiments are then added.

Zhu consists of boiling the seaweed in water – it is used principally to make soup. Frequently the seaweed is torn into small pieces, then other ingredients such as chopped fresh onions and parboiled noodles are added before water is poured on.

Xian (or filling) involved combining seaweed with meat or chopped vegetables, along with soy sauce, sesame oil, ginger and green onions, to make a filling or stuffing for dumplings which are fried, steamed or boiled, depending on the dough used.[18]

Chinese fried seaweed dumplings, served on a bed of seaweed.

introduced visitors to Chinese cuisine. Diners grappled with chopsticks while they worked their way through a menu that included *souchée* of salmon eaten with a delicate violet seaweed, washed down with hot Shaosing wine.[19] The exhibition menu was a pale reflection of the repasts served daily to the then ruler of China, the Empress Dowager Cixi (Tzu Hsi, 1835–1908). In the imperial palace, two main meals were served to the Empress daily, each consisting of 48 seasonal dishes containing ingredients selected to optimize health and flavour, including choice seaweeds.[20]

As in Japan, the most commonly eaten seaweeds in China today are *wakame*, *kan bu* (kombu or kelp) and *Porphyra* (nori), but in total at least 74 species are eaten or used, giving the Chinese a wide repertoire of edible algae.[21] There is not one Chinese cuisine, but many regional ones, and it is the seven coastal provinces and their cities that are known for seaweed dishes. Hong Kong has several seaweed specialities, reflecting the fact that it was one of the places where local seaweed species grew well, until urbanization took its toll on the local waters.[22] Shanghai is renowned for its 'seaweed fish' – deep-fried fish fillets in batter to which shredded seaweed has been added, giving a wonderful colour and flavour – and for seaweed fried rice as well as baked pastry buns with a sweet-sour seaweed filling. The 'crispy seaweed' popular in Cantonese-style restaurants is often not seaweed at all, but fried green cabbage, a misnomer that is more than made up for by dishes such as Cantonese seaweed spring rolls and long-simmered seaweed soup. In Guangdong, which has hot and humid summers, the cooling qualities of seaweed have been elaborated into a repertoire of dishes based on agar, which is cut

A simple and effective way of using seaweed, powdered and sprinkled over China's great comfort food – congee or rice porridge – to give it savour.

into cubes of jelly and added to fruit salads or chopped into strips which serve as 'noodles' in cold soups, while Fujian is known for its succulent omelette-cakes of oysters and seaweed, and Guizhou is renowned for its seaweed pancakes.

Across China, there are many ways of eating *Laminaria* (*konbu* or *kan bu*):

> made into a substantial soup with pork; cut into thin strips and boiled with beaten egg to make 'egg flower' soup; layering the seaweed with fish in a pressure cooker with soy sauce, vinegar, sugar, spring onions, oil and a dash of Chinese wine and cooking for an hour under pressure, or for longer over low heat if not using a pressure cooker. A large piece of kelp can have a layer of pork, soy sauce, sugar, green onions and salt spread on it, then the whole is rolled up, steamed or stewed, and cut into bite-sized pieces.[23]

Dishes made from *Sargassum fusiforme*, well-regarded since ancient times, are also popular, either mixed with oil and spring onion as a filling for dumplings; stir-fried with mussels; cooked with bean curd in a dish called *sha dou fu*; or mixed with brown sugar to make a sweet filling for steamed buns eaten at New Year and other important festivals.[24]

Seaweed was primarily an expensive import until the fall of the Chinese monarchy in 1912.[25] This was followed by two decades of civil war until the establishment of the People's Republic of China in 1949 under Mao Zedong. Then began a series of 'reforms' such as the Great Leap Forward that lasted almost thirty years. Severe austerity measures were introduced, including the periodic banning of imported goods and luxuries such as seaweed. There were some efforts to farm seaweed by planting on the seabed or growing it from floating

Tung Cheng-yi, *Commune Fishpond*, 1973, mariculture in the Mao era.

rafts, as part of a commitment to increasing the consumption of aquatic foods in order to relieve pressure on the land, but success was limited.[26]

Agricultural land and labour were sacrificed to industrial development, which led to widespread, severe famines, and by the time Mao died in 1976 the economy and national health were in ruins. Realizing both had to be rebuilt, Mao's successors mandated urgent increases in food production. While land resources were overstretched, the China seas had not been intensively developed. Looking at Japan's post-war success with seaweed, China entered the commercial seaweed farming market in earnest, aiming to generate export revenue and improve the diet of the Chinese people. The results were dramatic. In 1980 China produced 262,000 metric tons of seaweed; in 2005 that figure was 1,542,000 metric tons,[27] and today, China is the world's largest producer of edible seaweed. Onshore, traditional Chinese medicine flourishes and with it the medicinal use of seaweed, and the Chinese are actively researching the biomedical uses of seaweed in the Western tradition. Unlike Japan, where seaweed has been at the heart of daily eating habits for millennia, seaweed availability on the present scale is relatively recent in China, so Chinese seaweed cuisine can be seen as a tasty work in progress.

Seaweed in Korea

While visiting Korea in the 1890s, the intrepid Victorian lady traveller Isabella Bird saw seaweed everywhere from the moment her ship landed at the treaty port of Wonsan – piles of it in markets and bundles of dried fish and seaweed – 'the latter a great article of diet' – carried up to the city of Seoul on the backs of coolies. Seaweed was part of the basic soup and noodle meals offered in roadside inns and eating houses, and it was an ingredient of the meals of labourers – she commented particularly on a dish of salted seaweed fried in batter.[28]

Elizabeth Keith, an eating house in old Korea, like those seen by the Victorian traveller Isabella Bird.

Although seaweed also figured in imperial cuisine, Bird did not experience it when she was invited to dine at the palace. On that occasion, as a compliment to the guest, all the food, from stuffed and rolled beef to glacé walnuts, was cooked in the 'foreign style'. And so she missed partaking of *gungjung-eumsik*, the royal cuisine of the Joseon Dynasty that has since been revived and declared an 'Important Intangible Cultural Property' by the Korean state, in which some 24 refined dishes would have been served at each main meal in the palace, always including seaweed soup.[29]

With China on one side and Japan on the other, peninsular Korea has always struggled to maintain its political independence and culinary identity, having spent much of the last two millennia caught between these powerful neighbours, to whom it has long supplied seaweed from its clear and cold waters, both as tribute and as trade. For centuries Chinese influence was dominant, but at the time of Bird's visit Japan was in the ascendance, culminating in the occupation of Korea by Japan between 1910 and 1945, during which time Korean court traditions, including high cuisine, were set aside.[30] Korea became 'the rice bowl of the Japanese Empire', producing food to support Japan's expansion.[31] The Japanese encouraged commercial cultivation of nori, called *gim* in Korea, to supplement traditional wild harvesting; introduced Japanese production methods; and promoted eating in the Japanese style, which was resisted by the Koreans. As a result, while there are some superficial similarities, the Koreans are always keen to point out how their food differs from that of Japan and of China, nori sheets – which the Japanese taught the Koreans to produce on a large scale – being a prime example.

The flavour of nori sheets can be enhanced by lightly brushing them with an oil or liquid and then briefly toasting them: the Japanese like to use soy for this purpose, while

Tray of *gimbap*, the Korean version of *norimaki*.

the Koreans prefer to use sesame oil. A favourite traditional Korean speciality is deep fried laver, which is made by applying a sticky glue-like paste made of cooked rice to sheets of laver. When the coated sheets are dry they are deep fried, producing a crunchy snack similar to potato crisps, but with a wonderful savoury flavour. Koreans do not share the Japanese passion for wrapping, which requires quite firm and thick sheets. Instead, they prefer lighter, lacier nori sheets, which they consider more attractive and delicious. When they do make nori-wrapped foods, the Korean approach is distinctive. *Gimbap* is the Korean version of *norimaki*, and while it does use thicker nori, *gimbap* is more robust in appearance and includes more generous fillings than Japanese sushi – differences the practised eye and palate can soon detect.

Although *gimbap* has become more popular as a result of the globalization of sushi, the Koreans still prefer to shred and sprinkle their lacy *gim* over food, notably in one of the most popular Korean dishes, *bibimbap*. This is a one-bowl dish of cooked rice, cooked vegetables, beef and an egg, brought to the table in a hot bowl and mixed together just before eating, giving a fresher taste than Chinese fried rice, as the Koreans like to point out.

Since the 1970s, Korea has sought to reaffirm its national identity through promoting its culture and particularly the distinctive features of its cuisine. Everyday Korean cuisine is pungent, spicy and heady, its three favourite flavourings – sesame, garlic and chilli – accentuated by four fermented ingredients: *doenjang* (soybean paste), *ganjang* (soy sauce), *jeotgal* (fish sauce) and *gochujang* (chilli paste).[32] Although chilli is a New World plant that was only introduced to Korea through Western contact around the sixteenth century, it is impossible to imagine contemporary Korean cuisine without it, particularly as it is the key ingredient in kimchi, the piquant and strongly flavoured pickled vegetables that embody 'Korean-ness' to outsiders and to the Koreans themselves. Fiery kimchi is usually made with cabbage, but a variety of vegetables can be used, and piquant flavours find their way into many Korean seaweed preparations. Kelp is used as a wrap for rice and other foods; it is dipped into pickled anchovy sauce; simmered

Uniquely Korean – sushi made with kimchi.

in soy with strips of dried fish; boiled and served cold with chilli pepper paste; or deep fried as a side dish or snack. By comparison, Korean cuisine can make both Japanese and Chinese food seem bland.

Like China, Korea intensified its commercial seaweed farming after the Second World War. Its production of nori benefited greatly – like the Japanese – from the scientific discoveries of Kathleen Drew-Baker (see Chapter Two). Today, Korea is the second-largest producer of commercial seaweed and the Koreans have carved out a niche as innovators in the flavoured seaweed snack market, drawing on their palette of intense flavours.

In addition to its pungent taste, Korean cuisine has a distinctive style that can best be described as 'rustic' and 'natural' – earthy rather than elegant as epitomized by Japanese foodways, and simple and direct compared to the complexity of Chinese cookery. The Koreans have their own saying, *umsigi kut yagi toenta* – 'food is medicine'[33] – and believe that for them wellness is embodied in wild-gathered foods and those

Bibimbap, the popular Korean dish topped with shredded seaweed.

Korean *miyeok* soup with white rice, kimchi and seaweed salad.

produced on Korean lands and in Korean waters, prepared in the Korean way. Seaweed epitomized the love of the rustic that was celebrated in aristocratic circles and court poetry since antiquity. At the time of Bird's visit, the king and queen of Korea 'would sometimes retire to their version of the Petit Trianon, a huge old farmhouse built in a corner of the Secret Gardens of the Summer Palace in Seoul where they would relax with simple meals of grain, herbs and seaweed cooked by the queen's own hands,'[34] and listen to poetry, like this passage from the fourteenth-century *Song of the Green Mountain*:

> I shall live, I shall live I say
> I shall live by the sea.
> I shall eat oysters and clams and the seaweeds
> and live, I say, by the sea.
> *Yalli yalli yallasyŏng, yallari yalla.*[35]

The essence of Korea's love of seaweed can be seen in its *miyeok*, seaweed soup. In traditional Korean cuisine, soup is served at every meal and there is a vast repertoire among which seaweed soups have a special place. While Japanese soup can be so understated that the presence of seaweed can barely be detected, and Chinese seaweed soups are awash with many ingredients, Korean seaweed soup is elemental in its strength and simplicity. There are several types of Korean seaweed soup: chilled seaweed soup (*miyeok-naengguk*), made of blanched fresh seaweed to which soy and julienned cucumbers are added, and spicy seaweed soup (*miyeok-muchim*), blanched fresh seaweed seasoned with soy, vinegar and red chilli paste, but the key soup is known simply as *miyeok*. Made of dried seaweed (*wakame*) that is soaked, drained and then cooked in broth, *miyeok* is traditionally given to new mothers to build up their strength after childbirth. A pretty folktale says that the custom originated in antiquity after people had seen whales eat seaweed after giving birth. Whether or not they do eat it postpartum, in Korea as in Japan, whales symbolize long life. The association between the health represented by seaweed and the long life through the links with whales makes *miyeok* a highly symbolic and protective food, as well as a nutritious one. This is why new mothers eat it, why it is customary for everyone to have *miyeok* on their birthdays to protect them in the coming year, and why seaweed soup was served to the king and queen every day in the royal palace, to safeguard their health and longevity. This delicious soup is also a magical concoction.

4

Seaweed in the Pacific and the Americas

To sail across the Pacific, as the Polynesians did when they peopled the islands of Hawaii, Samoa, Tonga, Tahiti, Fiji, Aotearoa (New Zealand) and Rapa Nui (Easter Island), is to enter an area that does not appear in commercial seaweed statistics. With the exception of New Zealand and Easter Island, the South and equatorial Pacific are too warm to support the great cold water seaweeds like giant kelp, and in those places where a well-known species like *Porphyra* does grow, it tends to be both small and uncommon, and is not exported. However, many tropical seaweeds flourish in the Pacific islands, where they played an important part in traditional eating, and remain a culinary speciality, being relatively tender and delicate, and easy to prepare and eat raw. While there are differences between the Pacific island groups, Hawaii was where seaweed eating was and remains the most elaborate.

Seaweed in Hawaii

Although they appear to be verdant paradise islands where no effort is required to make fruit fall from the trees, plants spring from the land and fish leap into nets, the islands of

Polynesia are finely balanced ecosystems that demand constant management – part of which involved food taboos. Before Western contact, the range of food resources was limited. The land was planted in rotation to avoid exhausting the soil, and fish could only be taken during certain seasons to conserve stocks. The heaviest burden fell on the islands' women. To ensure the food supply, all women, from members of the elite to the common people, were forbidden to eat the finest foods – pigs, coconuts, turtles, most kinds of banana and the choicest fish – which were reserved for men. All Polynesian societies had food taboos, but those of Hawaii were the most extreme. The taboo was rigorously enforced and the penalty for transgression was death.[1] Women were also forbidden to plant, cultivate, prepare or cook food. Everything was done by the men, who delivered the food to the women but could not eat with them. The women ate together and the only kind of food provisioning they were allowed to do was to collect seaweed and shellfish, which became very important in their restricted diet, and which they turned into a high culinary art.

In the great Hawaiian creation chant, the *Kumulipo*, which recounts the origins of life, seaweed was one of the first things to be brought into being, to protect and nourish all the fish and humans which would later appear. Up to two hundred different kinds of tropical seaweeds or *limu* were recognized in Hawaii, and each section of the coast on all of the islands was known for the kind that grew well there.[2] Sometimes favourite seaweeds would be transplanted from one island to another, and grown in special 'seaweed gardens' for the benefit of the elite. Fish also profited from Hawaiian seaweed expertise. The Hawaiians had an advanced system of fish aquaculture, raising choice fish such as mullet in specially constructed ponds. These fish fed on microalgae, so the Hawaiians encouraged the growth of these plants in the ponds, as living

Frank MacIntosh, menu cover designed for the Matson Line cruise
ships, 1930s.

Sea turtle, now a protected species in Hawaii, eating *limu palahalaha,* sea lettuce, which the Hawaiians like to chop and mix with *opihi,* small molluscs.

fish foods.[3] Most seaweeds were gathered in the wild, and certain kinds were reserved for the elite, such as *Asparagopsis taxiformis*, known in Hawaii as *limu kohu*. Women did the harvesting and tending, but men were allowed to share in the rewards. As this old Hawaiian riddle put it:

My little fish without entrails,
But alive, is very good to eat,
And is greatly desired by chiefs and common people,
What am I?
The seaweed.[4]

The daily food of the common people was fish, *poi* (pounded taro) and *limu*, which acted as a tasty relish. Seaweed could be pounded, boiled, baked, dried or crushed.[5] Although some kinds were allowed to ferment slightly to deepen the flavour, or soaked in seawater for a day to lessen the iodine taste, seaweeds were usually eaten fresh soon after picking, either on their own as a relish for bland sweet potatoes or taro, or chopped up and mixed with fish or the abundant shellfish and seafood in different combinations – one kind was always mixed with octopus, another with *opihi*, a small mollusc, and there were many other pairings of particular fish, raw or cooked, with specific seaweeds. A favourite relish was *inamona*, made from *kukui* or candlenuts, chopped fine and mixed with seaweed and salt; a Western visitor reported that it 'resembles Russian caviar in flavour – the Hawaiians serve this with poi (mashed taro), raw or cooked fish, or roast meats'.[6] Even when the food taboos were abolished in 1819, the passion for seaweed eating continued, and every morning as the tides went out women could be seen picking seaweed on the reefs and shore, as celebrated in this traditional chant:

Such a delight it is to see
The great big ocean
So familiar and very cherished
With its fragrance of the *lipoa* (seaweed).

How enticing is the display of *limu kohu*
Atop the rocks in the ocean
Enticing one to pick them
As they sway to and fro.[7]

Seaweeds continue to be prized and sold in the local markets in Hawaii, and there is now also a global dimension to seaweed eating in Hawaii because of the islands' cosmopolitan culture. People from Japan, Korea, China, the Philippines, the South Pacific and Southeast Asia emigrated to Hawaii in the nineteenth and twentieth centuries, bringing their seaweed cuisines with them, later adapting them to island ways. The Koreans make kimchi with Hawaiian seaweed, and the Japanese prepare their agar *kanten* jellies with coconut milk rather than with citrus yuzu and green tea. Some American adaptations are popular in the islands. *Limu lepoa* (*Dictyopteris australis*) is sometimes used in martinis in place of an olive,[8] and seaweed is a popular flavouring for popcorn.

Hawaii consumes more Spam – a canned pork product made by the Hormel Foods Corporation – than any other state in America. Many ways of eating it are enjoyed in the islands, but the most popular is Spam *musube*. In this dish, the basic Japanese *musube*, a ball of white rice partially wrapped in sheets of nori, is topped with a slice of Spam that has been lightly fried in soy sauce – a simple snack that is regarded by locals as one of the delights of island cuisine.

Another element in the island seaweed repertoire is Filipino cuisine, which was influenced by Spanish, Malay and Chinese cookery before it reached Hawaii. One popular

A fusion snack from Hawaii, seaweed-flavoured popcorn.

Spam *musube*, a much-loved local speciality in Hawaii.

Filipino speciality of Asian origins is *lumpia*, which can be fried like spring rolls or steamed like dumplings – both have stuffings that combine vegetables, seafood or meat with chopped seaweed. *Guisado* is a braised or sautéed dish with colonial roots, consisting of rice, vegetables, fruit, fish or meat, with chopped seaweed to thicken it and to add extra flavour.

But for locals and visitors alike, the great island favourite is based on the old Hawaiian way of preparing seaweed known as *poke* – chopped fresh seaweed mixed with chopped raw fish, molluscs or cooked octopus, garnished with more seaweed and chilli pepper, with red Hawaiian *alaea* salt to sprinkle over. *Poke* – pronounced poh-kay – has become a cult food for fish and seaweed connoisseurs and *poke* festivals are held in Hawaii, California and Japan.

Hawaiian *ahi limu poke*, made here with tuna.

The Hawaiians loved proverbs and sayings, many involving seaweed. A chief who was renowned for being handsome and kind was described as *limu nui*, meaning that women fell in love with him as easily as gathering seaweed. But not all references to seaweed were positive. Hawaiians used to say that a person of weak character was like a sea lettuce, easily swayed by the action of the tides, while they compared aimless people who merely drift to seaweed washed up upon the shore.[9]

Seaweeds were also used in traditional Hawaiian healing. Certain seaweeds were used to treat conditions such as chest pain, rashes, backache and alimentary disorders, and also in healing rituals. *Limu kala* (*Sargassum echinocarpum*) was especially important. One of the meanings of *kala* is 'to loosen' or 'to free'. Since it was believed that sickness was caused by evil spirits, and a patient could not be free from illness until the spirits had left the body, a *lei* or garland of *limu kala* was made for the patient, who would put it around his or her neck and swim out to sea. When the garland floated away, it took the spirits and the illness with it. Another meaning of *kala* is 'forgiveness'. The Hawaiians had a form of family therapy called *ho'oponopono* in which members gathered in a circle to discuss grievances and resolve problems. At the end of the session, as part of the healing ritual, everyone ate *limu kala*.[10] The seaweed *limu ko'ele'ele* (*Gymnogongrus* sp.) was said to have powerful aphrodisiac properties when eaten, but only when accompanied by a certain chant.[11] Sadly, that chant does not seem to have survived.

Seaweed on the Pacific Northwest Coast

North by northeast from Hawaii, one connects again with the Pacific Great Kelp Highway and the many fish, sea mammals and other living things it supports. These were waters travelled by the English explorer Captain James Cook on his third and final voyage in 1778. After reaching present-day Oregon, he sailed as far north as the Bering Strait, traversing a coast described by his men as brooding and melancholy, with impenetrable forests of tall, dark cedar trees and steep precipices that plunged down to a rocky shore.[12] The Pacific coasts of Canada and the American states of Washington and Oregon are home to the great seaweed cultures of the Pacific Northwest, peoples like the Tlingit, the Haida, the Kwakwaka'wakw (Kwakiutl), the Gitga'at, the Nuu-chah-nulth (Nootka) and others who lived in villages hugging the water's edge, in houses facing the sea, fronted by carved totem poles.[13]

Early accounts describe the rich marine resources of the area which were supported by the kelp: several sorts of whales and seals, orcas, sea otters, walruses and sea lions supplemented in summer by the five kinds of salmon that came to spawn, as well as by abundant halibut, cod, herring and olachen (*Thaleichthys pacificus*). Clams, cockles, mussels and other shellfish were plentiful and there were bountiful supplies of seaweeds. The coastal people were primarily hunter-fisher-gatherers whose main diet was the meat of sea mammals and fish, supplemented by local berries, land plants and seaweed. Life depended on the sea, and seaweed was at the very heart of Pacific Northwest culture, not just to eat but to use. Traditionally, bull kelp was used for fishing lines up and down the coast. The kelp stems were soaked in fresh water, twisted to make them strong and then tied together with a special knot for length.[14] Bull kelp stems were also used to make nets, ropes, harpoon and anchor lines, and served as storage containers for fish oil and other items. Young kelp stems and bulbs were pickled and also eaten fresh.[15]

A number of seaweeds were gathered, including sea lettuce, but the favoured seaweed for eating was the 21 species of *Porphyra* which grow there.[16] *Porphyra* was picked in a systematic manner, sometimes from 'seaweed camps' set up for the purpose near to good picking beds, with each group having its agreed or at least shared territory. There was no 'spot-picking' as in contemporary foraging; good beds were treated like gardens, worked regularly to make the seaweed grow stronger and better, maximizing sustainability.[17] Under ideal conditions, two pickings of seaweed could be harvested from a site in the same year, with the taste of the second growth reckoned to be finer.[18] Picking seaweed was women's work, and just as fishermen had to be alert at sea, so seaweed picking demanded knowledge of the treacherous tides and currents of the coast and shore.

Once picked, the seaweed was spread out to dry, and it was vital that it was not rained on. Once thoroughly dry, the seaweed would be shaped and cured, or otherwise preserved, by methods that varied slightly along the coast. The Gitxsan packed dried seaweed sprinkled with salt water and layered with cedar bark or local plant leaves into cedar boxes, which were then weighted and left to mature, producing blocks of dried, cured seaweed that could be stored or used in trade with people who lived inland. They also dried and chopped it and put it into large containers, only taking out the amount they needed so as to avoid exposing the seaweed to the air, which changed its colour and flavour. The Kwakiutl said that seaweed should not be dried immediately, but should be kept under a mat for a few days to ferment slightly and become more tender. Then it was put onto racks of split cedar to

Bull kelp on the beach, Vancouver Island, British Columbia.

Traditional Pacific Northwest Coast method of cooking salmon, for which seaweed was a customary accompaniment.

allow it to dry in the sun and wind. They packed dried seaweed into cedar boxes to mature and cured it by a fire, toasting it on specially made cedar frames. When the seaweed was browned, it was beaten into a powder, put into a tightly covered container and stored in a dry place in the house.[19] Further north in Alaska, the seaweed was chopped, mixed with seal oil and stored in a seal bladder.[20]

There were many ways of cooking the seaweed. One Kwakiutl method was to cut the seaweed into smaller strips, chew them slightly, put them into a kettle, boil for some time and then add fish oil. The seaweed was ready when the oil had been absorbed. This could be eaten morning, noon or night, but in the morning it was customary to eat dried fish, salmon or halibut before eating the seaweed. Powdered

Cedar box, *c.* 1875, of the kind used to store dried seaweed
on the Pacific Northwest Coast, Haida peoples.

Alaskan herring roe on a piece of kelp from Sitka, Alaska, a local delicacy that is also exported to Japan.

seaweed was eaten in the same way. People ate directly from the small kettle, and stones were added to keep the mixture hot, because it was not considered good to eat when cold. Another popular dish was clams and seaweed boiled together. Abalone, cockles and salmon eggs – which were as well regarded as caviar – were prepared in a similar way.[21] One of the great traditional delicacies along the coast and up into Alaska was seaweed upon which fish had laid their spawn. This continues to be highly prized locally, and in Japan, where it is exported as roe-on-kelp or *komochi konbu*.

Seaweed was also used in earth-oven cooking. A hole was dug, lined with stones, and a fire lit in it. When ready the hot stones in the pit are levelled and a thin layer of soil is placed on top, then a layer of seaweed. The food to be cooked is put in, more layers of leaves, branches and seaweed are added, and a mat is put over the hole. Finally, water is added and the food is left to steam overnight. A similar technique was used to make a medicinal steam bath, when hot stones and seaweed were laid in a long cedar box, with the patient – wrapped in blankets – laid upon it to inhale the vapours.[22] Seaweed had other medicinal applications and leisure uses: at Fort Rupert on Vancouver Island and elsewhere, dried seaweed was 'carried and chewed in much the same way as tobacco'.[23]

In the Pacific Northwest seaweed formed part of a traditional diet that was healthy and balanced compared to modern fare, which is heavily dependent on processed food and starches. These have impacted negatively on health and wellness, and non-sustainable commercial activities threaten the coastal marine ecosystem. Protection of the local environment, restoration of traditional food systems, food sovereignty and holistic healthy eating are high on the agenda of First Nations' councils and people, and central to this is the encouragement of seaweed consumption adapted to modern life.

New domestic techniques include chopping seaweed in food processors and drying it in a pillowcase in a clothes dryer;[24] there are lessons for young people on sustainable seaweed harvesting and First Nations cookbooks that combine heritage, health and good eating in a contemporary style with dishes such as seaweed-stuffed baked salmon, broiled salmon with pickled seaweed, fish and seaweed chowder and pan-fried kelp with roe, in a style epitomized by the acclaimed Mitsitam Native Foods Café at the National Museum of the American Indian in Washington, DC.[25]

Seaweed Heading South

The Great Kelp Highway continues down the Pacific coast as far south as northern California, where great pyramids of mollusc shells – a testament of long-ago shellfish feasts left by the coastal California Indians – were a striking feature of the landscape until flattened in modern times for development. To many, the region of southern California is synonymous with Mexican food, but there was a delicious northern and central indigenous California cuisine that included fish, shellfish and sun-dried seaweed, which was eaten and traded inland. Mendocino, a prime collecting site for the Native Californians, is a centre of seaweed harvesting today.[26]

Cal-Mex (California Mexican) innovations include fish or seafood tacos – sometimes described as 'Japanese burritos' – wrapped in nori instead of tortillas, and seaweed guacamole. California was an early adopter of Japanese sushi, but has developed its own variations. For those who do not want to bother with rolling nori sheets, there is California-style pan sushi – rice pressed into a pan and then sprinkled over the top with *furikake nori* (a mixture of shaved bonito, powdered

Seaweed tacos, an example of Cal-Mex cuisine.

California pan sushi.

nori and sesame) – with a dipping sauce of ponzu (citrus and soy) and wasabi mayonnaise served on the side.

The Kelp Highway stops when it hits the warm waters off Mexico and Central America, resuming at the latitude of Peru. Several kinds of seaweed were part of the diet of the ancient Incas, and runners used to carry balls of dried seaweed from the coast up to Cuzco, the capital high in the Andes, for the use of the Inca ruler and the elite. Today seaweed appears in many forms in the newly fashionable Peruvian cuisine, notably in the Peruvian signature dish, ceviche, that uses the fine local seafood. Further south lies Chile, where Monte Verde and its cache of nine ancient seaweeds that rewrote prehistory, as discussed in Chapter One, were discovered. Seaweed eating in Chile continues: the favoured species are bull kelp (*Durvillaea antarctica*, commonly called *cochayuyo*), which was also found in Monte Verde, and *luche*, a species of *Porphyra*.

Seaweed as sold in the markets of Chile, dried bull kelp, *cochayuyo*, and bags of dried *luche* (*Porphyra*). The dried *luche* is also pressed into cakes.

Bull kelp is tough, requiring lengthy cooking to make it edible. When the Spanish conquistador Cortéz Ojea arrived in 1558, he found the natives preparing kelp, writing:

> we roasted the hard stems like fat radishes, in the ashes to make them more tender, and then we put them on to boil in small pieces like fingers, five or six hours; we added flour and mashed them well, then returned them to the pots and cooked them an hour with limpets and shellfish.[27]

Once having mastered the preparation of *cochayuyo*, the conquistadors used it in a variety of colonial dishes that have become part of Chile's culinary heritage: *cochayuyo* empanadas, lamb stew with *cochayuyo* and *cochayuyo* and potato stew.[28] *Cochayuyo* can also be cooked, mixed with vegetables, dressed with oil and lime and eaten as a salad.

At the southernmost tip of South America, facing Antarctica, lies Tierra del Fuego – desolate and demanding, surrounded by the cold seas thick with kelp written about by Darwin during his voyage on the *Beagle*. Here, where frost lies on the ground from one year to the next, there developed a fishing, hunting and foraging culture based upon seaweed. The coastal peoples lived on the products of the sea: fish, shellfish – particularly huge mussels – seals, sea lions, whales, otters and sea birds, all of which were dependent on the kelp. At sea, kelp was central to the food quest; kelp helped to

Chilean cooked *cochayuyo* salad.

launch canoes drawn up on the beach, and once at sea the canoes were moored to the floating kelp while the people fished using lines made of kelp. On shore, kelp was at the centre of everyday life, used to make the roofs and walls of houses, mattresses, clothing and storage bags. Small shellfish grew on the kelp, which the women stripped for food, and, in an environment with few plants, kelp and other cold-water seaweeds were an essential food resource for the natives as well as for their prey.

It was a hard life but the coastal peoples seen by Darwin thrived until they succumbed to infectious diseases after Western contact. However, their perfect adaptation to a seaweed environment was not forgotten. In the early twentieth century, during the great age of Antarctic exploration, the British explorer Sir Ernest Shackleton's expeditions were trapped in the ice on several occasions, and were forced to fall back on native foodways to survive. During the expedition of 1907–9, they were sustained by a strong blizzard that cast a quantity of seaweed upon the ice, which they considered a piece of great good fortune. During the expedition of 1914–17, their supplies had to be eked out with local foraging – as one crew member recorded, 'the soup was particularly good that day, consisting of boiled seal's backbone, limpets and seaweed.'[29] In the end, supplies ran out and the men were reduced to digging up buried seal bones from previous meals and boiling them for a second or third time. It was the seaweed which sustained them until they were rescued. In fact, they were boiling up some seaweed and limpet soup when they spotted the ship that had come to save them, knocking over the precious pot as they sprang up and ran for the shore.

Irish Moss – The Caribbean Aphrodisiac

Midway between the kelp forests of the cold north and south, the warm waters of the Caribbean have many features in common with Hawaii. In the islands, tropical seaweeds are consumed locally, as they were by the pre-colonial Caribs and Arawaks. One kind of seaweed found in the Caribbean and elsewhere – *Chondrus crispus* – has gained wide renown as an aphrodisiac when prepared in the Caribbean manner, thought to have been adapted from colonial dishes. Also known as 'Irish moss', *Chondrus crispus* is a source of carrageenan, which is used as a thickening agent in processed foods and in traditional cooking. Described as a 'man's drink', the theory is that just as carrageenan stiffens food, so it has a similar effect on the male member. The basic method is to take the dried moss, soak it overnight, boil it in water for about an hour until it is syrupy, then strain it and refrigerate overnight. The next day the moss liquid is mixed with condensed milk and flavourings such as nutmeg, vanilla and cinnamon, either by hand if the moss liquid is syrupy, or in a blender if it has gelled stiff. Rum is sometimes added, and the drink is so popular that it is available throughout the Caribbean, ready made in bottles and cans.

The 'New England' Clam Bake

Going up the Atlantic coast of the Americas, the kelp forests reappear in the cold waters off New England and Canada's Atlantic provinces. Early accounts of the coastal regions where the first explorers and colonists landed portray a bounteous foodscape of game, fowl, fruits, vegetables and, above all, fish. 'There is no country known,' wrote William

Wood in 1634, 'that yields more variety of fish, winter and summer,'[30] going on to describe whales, cod, halibut, hake, the favoured sea bass, turbot, sturgeon, smaller sorts and what he called 'fish without shells' – molluscs. Then, as now, these were the glory of the New England coast: oysters a foot long, mussels aplenty and above all clams, some as large as a penny loaf of bread. There were fine lobsters too, the largest near to 9 kg (20 lbs) in weight, so numerous that they were used as bait for fishing. The natives were well aware of the marine wealth they possessed, as John Smith wrote in 1616, 'comparing their store in the sea to the hairs on their head'.[31] Although glowing accounts of the New World were written to attract colonists and investors, the marine resources of the New England coast were not overstated, with one exception – seaweed.

The coasts of northern New England and Canada are among the most productive seaweed habitats in the world, with kelp, rockweed, sea lettuce, Irish moss and other species growing in abundance, supporting the flora, fauna and people of the coast. But because they were not reckoned by the early colonists to have any commercial potential, seaweeds were not described in their records except as a nuisance, or as thatching for roofs until better materials could be obtained.

The Wampanoag, the First Nations people whose home territory stretched from Cape Cod to Narragansett Bay in southeastern Massachusetts, exemplified the Eastern Woodlands way of life, alternating between the coast and the interior, fully exploiting the resources of land and sea depending on the time of year. The women planted and harvested corn, beans and squash while the men hunted game. In the summer they moved to the coast, establishing camps from which they could fish and collect molluscs and lobsters. It was during their time at the shore, where seaweed was plentiful, that the Wampanoag held *appanaugs*.[32] Translated as 'seafood cooking',

'New England' clam bake, descended from Native American *appanaugs*.

appanaugs were feasts given to mark special events, using the earth-oven technique employed by many other First Nations people. A hole was dug and lined with stones and a fire of dry wood was kindled in it; when the fire burned down to ashes and the stones were hot, the pit was strewn with newly gathered rockweed (*Ascophyllum nodosum*), onto which were piled clams, lobsters and corn, which were then covered with more seaweed, and the whole was cooked by steam fragrant with the sea.

The Wampanoag were the people that the Pilgrims encountered when they arrived in the New World in 1620, and they taught the new arrivals many things, including how to fertilize the soil by burying dead fish when planting crops, ensuring the settlers' survival. However, they did not convert the newcomers to the *appanaug* because the early colonists were suspicious of First Nations cookery methods, other than boiling and roasting. They considered clams such poor food that they later fed them to the hogs and they had the conventional Western disdain for seaweed. There are no records of the early colonists attending *appanaugs*, yet ironically, in the nineteenth century, under the name 'clam bakes', they emerged as a culinary symbol of the nation's beginnings, emblematic of the hardships and successes of the first European settlers. Accepted as an 'authentic' colonial practice, clam bakes became a patriotic fixture of the New England lifestyle – the cult activity of the area as the barbecue is in other places, considered as American as the Fourth of July.[33] Controversy rages about whether or not potatoes should be included or if the cooked shellfish should be dipped in melted butter, but there is agreement on one thing – for a real clam bake, as opposed to a 'boil', seaweed is essential.

There are fashions in clam bakes, as in all things culinary, but here are instructions for a classic Cape Cod clam bake from 1949, in which potatoes do not appear.[34] It may not be properly colonial, but the *appanaug* or clam bake is authentically First Nations, making seaweed part of America's earliest culinary history and heritage.

Following the failure of the potato harvest in Ireland in 1845, there was substantial emigration to America, with many Irish ending up in New England, particularly in Massachusetts. They brought their foodways with them, one of which was the harvest, sale and culinary use of Irish moss or carrageen. There are plenty of carrageen recipes in Boston Irish cookery, especially for puddings and for stews thickened with carrageen. Spotting the abundance of carrageen in the local waters, the Irish set up seaweed-harvesting businesses – called mossing – which thrived until the 1970s, when they were driven out of business by cheap imports from the Far East.[35]

Make a round bed of stones on the ground, field or beach rock or any type of stones availawble, the best about as large as a cabbage. Cover an area about a yard in diameter, and crown about a foot high. Stack firewood on top, and keep feeding the fire steadily as it burns for at least four hours. Rake away all charred wood and embers, leaving just the heated stones. Then cover with a heavy layer (6 or 8 inches) of rockweed or seaweed.

Meanwhile prepare the food to be cooked:

Lobsters: Take a large square of cheesecloth and lay 3 or 4 side by side. Tie and knot the 4 corners together. This makes it easy to remove bundle later from hot seaweed.

Corn: Corn should be stripped to the last two layers of husk. 3 or 4 ears to a bundle, the same as the lobsters.

Broilers, fish etc. are also used: Tie them all in the same way, and cut to lay flat. If clams, oysters or mussels are also to be baked, wash well in sea water to remove all sand or mud and do not tie them.

Arrangement: Leave space in center, and use circular arrangement for placing food, for attractive bake. Start inner circle with alternate bundles of corn and lobster, side by side. The same circle arrangement of other foods. And last, on the outer edges (where the heat is less intense) place the shell fish, clams, oysters or mussels, etc.

Now cover all with a 4 or 6 inch layer of seaweed. Next cover the entire pile with a piece of canvas large enough to extend over the ground and be fastened down tightly by placing rocks around the edges. This is important to prevent any steam from escaping.

Time of bake: Allow a full 45 minutes. Then remove the canvas, and top layer of seaweed. The bake is very colourful and picturesque if foods have been artfully placed, the rich pinky red lobster being set off by the alternate bundles of light green corn in husks, etc, and the fringe of white clams about the outer edge, all combine to charm the eye and admiration of waiting guests. The luscious fragrance that wafts through the air as the bake is 'undone' is certain to linger long in the memory of all sea food gourmets.

Clams can be raked off the edges into small wooden bowls or cardboard pie plates. Keep a can of melted butter near the hot rocks, and small cardboard cups for individual servings of butter. Several tin salt shakers should also be provided.

Note: in buying broilers and lobsters, all should be of uniform size for uniform baking, a pound or 1½ lbs, not larger.

Full Clam Bake menu: Quahog (large clam) chowder served with golden pork scraps and toasted, buttered common crackers. Clams, lobster, corn etc, hot rolls. Blueberry or apple pie with vanilla ice cream. Coffee. Cokes for the young fry and iced beer for the grown-ups.

Moving beyond supplying seaweed for clam bakes and fertilizer and to the phycocolloid industry, there are now booming edible seaweed-harvesting enterprises on the east and west coasts of America, in areas where seaweed was gathered by First Nations people who also continue to eat it. There are several identifiable food traditions in the new American seaweed cookery: Japanese and Asian; fusion-style; vegetarian and macrobiotic; mainstream in which seaweed is added to standard dishes, including baked goods, soups and stews; and the downright funky, like the 'DLT' – the dulse, lettuce and tomato sandwich – that uses toasted or smoked dulse instead of bacon, which it tastes like.

During the nineteenth century, dulse eating was not widely taken up in America, although it was sometimes glimpsed in areas of heavy Irish immigration like Philadelphia. However, it became part of the culinary heritage of the Atlantic Maritime provinces of Canada, a destination for many Irish and Scottish immigrants, who brought their love of dulse with them, using it in cookery and even as a dummy (pacifier) for babies,[36] and dried dulse remains a popular snack there today.

Rich in seaweed and in fish, the Maritime provinces were and are home to the Micmac (Mi'kmaq) First Nations people, whose traditional diet included fish, shellfish, crustaceans and seaweeds, primarily dulse and kelp. They had their own version of the clam bake, but in the Maritimes among settlers it was more usual to boil shellfish and crustaceans rather than bake them, and when mussels were cooked the preferred method was to put them into a heavy iron boiler packed between layers of kelp, before filling the pot with seawater and boiling it for about twenty minutes.[37] The

American DLT sandwich: toasted or smoked dulse, lettuce and tomato.

Dulse harvesters – called 'dulsers' – in New Brunswick, Canada.

early settlers ate solid fishermen's fare, a cuisine of dried, salt or fresh cod and salmon with potatoes, salt pork and dried pulses, but today the Maritime provinces are a culinary tourism destination, drawing people for imaginative cookery based on the superb local fish and seafood from their clear, cold waters – a cuisine in which seaweed plays a role, notably in lobster, scallop or oyster chowders with dulse, and with fish and shellfish dishes of all kinds. Grand Manan Island in the Bay of Fundy is the centre of a flourishing seaweed harvest and export industry, and is known as the 'Dulse Capital of the World'.

Dulse stand, Saint John City Market, New Brunswick, Canada.

5
Seaweed in Ireland, Wales, England, Scotland and Scandinavia

Ireland, Wales and Scotland have long traditions of eating and using seaweed, with regional variations that are linked to local and national identity. Although misconceptions abound – such as the mistaken claim that seaweed was introduced to the British Isles as a survival food by the Vikings in the eighth century, or that it was only eaten during famines – its use is ancient. Generally it is possible to reconstruct an early coastal hunting-gathering-fishing lifestyle that included the gathering of nuts, berries, lichens and seaweeds. When agriculture was established in the coastal regions where the soil tended to be poor, seaweed was spread on the fields as fertilizer, like manure. This practice was long carried out all along the Atlantic coast, on the Scottish, North Sea and Channel Islands, in Brittany and further south. Largely discontinued in the twentieth century, it is now being revived in organic farming.

Because it was valuable, seaweed was usually not free for foraging: local lords and landowners zealously guarded their manorial rights and exacted payments from seaweed harvesters. Even today in Britain, permission to gather on the foreshore must be sought from the land's owners.[1] In

Gathering seaweed, called *vraic* locally, on Guernsey, one of the Channel Islands, for use as fertilizer in the late 19th century.

the past, lords and landowners gave important properties and rights to the Church to gain merit, which is how the Church became one of the largest owners and administrators of seaweed deposits, which they sold to farmers and used to fertilize their own monastery fields, which supported large communities of monks who also ate seaweed. In the sixth century, the Irish saint Brendan is said to have carried dried dulse or dillisk seaweed, which we now know is rich in vitamin C and protects against scurvy, to sustain him on his long voyages. On land the monks shared their seaweed bounty with the needy, as seen in the 'Prayer of St Columba' from a sixth-century psalter attributed to the Irish saint, who established an abbey on the Scottish island of Iona:

> Let me do my daily work
> Gathering dulse,
> Catching fish,
> Giving food to the poor.[2]

Seaweed in Ireland

But this prayer gives a rather dour view of seaweed consumption. Seaweed was a cherished food; the seventh-century Irish law text *Críth Gablach* set out rules of hospitality which stipulated that dulse was to be offered to people of status who came to one's door,[3] and in early medieval Ireland, where wealth was reckoned in cattle, shore access to a 'productive rock', meaning an outcrop with seaweed and shellfish, added three cows to the value of a land holding.[4]

Insight into the enjoyment offered by seaweed is seen in the great Irish narrative poem *The Vision of Mac Conglinne*, composed in the eleventh or twelfth century.[5] In it, the hero, having been given an inhospitable welcome at the monastery of Cork, has a vision of all the good things one could possibly want to eat, a glorious culinary vision in which appears a magical horse made entirely of food, with legs of custard, hoofs of bread, eyes of honey, a saddle of succulent corned beef cured with saltpetre made from burned seaweed, and a tail made of dulse from which seven handfuls could be pulled every day.

'Potatoes, children, seaweed': the old Irish saying about women's priorities captures the importance of seaweed in everyday life.[6] Ireland is seaweed-rich, with about five hundred species in its waters, which are plucked with great effort and danger 'from the jaws of the sea'.[7] Seaweed for fertilizing the fields was gathered from the rocky shore and taken off by donkey, or loaded onto bent shoulders. Rocky shores were hard going, but better than those on which the rocks were concealed under soft mud, into which the unwary could sink, breaking bones or becoming trapped in the face of the incoming tides. Small boats or currachs would go out to cut seaweed from offshore rocks; there was always the danger of capsizing if overloaded, and safe landing places along the western coast were rare. Gatherers had to watch the tides carefully in order to avoid getting swept out to sea or getting stranded on outlying rocks, and drowning. As one old seaweed harvester put it: 'Yes, the sea is always hungry, because a lot of people are always perishing in it.'[8]

The waters off Connemara on the west coast are rich in mayweed, oarweed, sea thong, bladderwrack, knotted wrack, sea oak, furbelows, sea belt, toothed and channelled wrack and more, which provided fertilizer and supported the kelp industry that flourished through the nineteenth century.[9] At that time, seaweed was burned in kilns along the coast to produce soda and iodine, providing essential income for coastal communities. Though diminished, 'kelping' persists in Ireland, and there is growing interest in seaweed for the burgeoning biochemical industries.

Dulse or dillisk (*Palmaria palmata*) and carrageen (*Chondrus crispus*) are the favourite edible seaweeds in Ireland.[10] Carrageen – also called Irish moss – is generally not eaten as a food, but is

Seaweed burning on the Irish coast, early 20th century.

Carrageen pudding served with stewed rhubarb, surrounded by dried carrageen.

usually gathered, dried and then boiled to extract a gelatinous substance that acts as a thickener and setting agent. On the west coast, carrageen is taken from the shore and outlying rocks at low tide, by pickers armed with creels, baskets, bags and buckets, standing half immersed in the cold water, 'harvesting with their two hands as hard as they can'.[11] Black when harvested, it is spread out to dry in the sun, where it turns red and then white. Today it is used as a hydrocolloid in processed foods and in other industrial applications, but originally it was used domestically to make sweet and savoury jellied puddings. Ireland was and is a great dairy country, and carrageen is the foundation of the milk puddings and blancmanges that are among the glories of traditional Irish cookery, as well as the basis of fruit gelatins and savoury mousses. It has found a new market today with vegans and vegetarians who cannot eat or use animal gelatin. Carrageen was also highly regarded in folk medicine, as a cure for coughs, sleeplessness, wheezing and dyspepsia, often administered as a hot drink boiled up with milk to which whiskey was sometimes added. These simple brews have been the inspiration for a new generation of designer cocktails and toddies, in a market always on the lookout for distinctive flavours and benefits – in this case, carrageen's subtle taste and its 'strengthening' qualities.

On the west coast of Ireland, people distinguish several sorts of red-brown dulse – the finest being *An Chreathnach*, 'shell dulse', upon which mussels grow and which is considered a great delicacy.[12] While the dulse is being harvested from the shore and outlying rocks between spring and autumn, pickers often chew on it as they go, both for the flavour and as a safeguard against illness. Once ashore, the dulse is dried so it will keep throughout the winter, a treasure of the larder used in many dishes to which its versatility lends itself, as it can be fried, boiled, grilled, stewed, chopped or ground and baked into bread, quiche or savoury biscuits. It can also be mixed with butter to make a rich and savoury spread. And people visiting friends and family in hospital used to take dulse for patients to nibble on, in much the same way that people elsewhere take presents of bunches of grapes.

A traditional favourite in Northern Ireland is dulse champ – potatoes mashed with milk and butter, to which chopped, cooked dulse is added at the end. As always with dried seaweed, soup is a popular means of reconstitution. *Cruasach*, which translates as 'health' or vigour', was a soupy stew made with seaweeds, including shell dulse, along with periwinkles and limpets – yet another example of the shellfish–seaweed pairing.[13] One simple century-old recipe involved stewing dulse with milk, butter, salt and pepper for three or four hours until tender, to be eaten with oatcakes or brown bread.[14] In contrast to this virtuous concoction, in Connemara 'heavy

'Irish Distress: Gathering Seaweed for Food on the Coast of Clare',
Illustrated London News, 1883.

drinkers make a soup of dulse so they can throw back a good
amount of drink without any effects. When the salt is dried
on it, it's a healthy thing to chew between drinks.'[15] Not just
popular with drinkers, dried dulse was and is a ubiquitous
snack, the original Irish street food, sold at markets, fairs and

above all at the races, as in this popular poem, 'The Caher-siveen Races':

> There were tents and umbrellas
> Where all kinds of fellows
> Sold dilisc and shellfish and the juicy crubeen
> And Peg's Legs the size of a peeler
> On the day of the races in Cahersiveen.[16]

But there is a sad passage in dulse's long history. When the potato crop failed, people from the interior came to the coast, hoping to keep alive by foraging. Some of the mussel heaps that are still to be seen in the west are not prehistoric, but date from those times of starvation. Dulse was their harvest of choice, although nearly anything was made to do, and the idea of seaweed as a famine food rather than as a valued part of the everyday Irish diet remains in the popular imagination as a ghostly legacy of those desperate days.

Seaweed in Wales

In Britain, the place most associated with seaweed eating is Wales, because of the Welsh love of laver (*Porphyra*), which was so much a part of traditional coastal culture that one of the characters in Dylan Thomas's drama *Under Milk Wood* wanted to know if it was also available in heaven, asking: 'How's it above? Is there rum and laverbread? Bosoms and robins?'[17]

Along the long Welsh coast, lapped by cold, clear waters, *Porphyra* grows in profusion, as seen in the village of Rhos-neigr, where Dr Kathleen Drew-Baker gathered the seaweed for her study that finally unravelled the mystery of the seaweed's life cycle in the 1930s. South Wales is also blessed with wide estuaries, which are home to the molluscs for which the area is known – cockles or small clams. Growing in close proximity, the seaweed and cockles are symbiotic. Drew-Baker's breakthrough discovery came through observing that the *Porphyra* spores thrived best when they settled on cockle shells on the seabed, which provided ideal growing conditions.

As often in coastal cultures, there was a division of labour between men and women: the men would fish, while the women collected seaweed and cockles. These were the 'web-footed cockle women' of *Under Milk Wood*, renowned for being very tough.[18] It was punishing work, the women frequently leaving home before sunrise, struggling barefoot along the shore and mudflats, avoiding quicksand and treacherous tides. Sackfuls of sea harvest were loaded onto donkeys or carts for the return journey, which was often made into a headwind with a rising tide at the women's backs. First the

The rocks at Rhosneigr, Wales, which provided the seaweed for Dr Kathleen Drew-Baker's breakthrough discovery of the life cycle of *Porphyra* and nori.

The 'web-footed cocklewomen' of South Wales, collectors of seaweed and shellfish in the late 19th century.

cockles were boiled in big cauldrons in sheds on the beach, then the laver – called 'the weed' by those who worked with it – would be cleaned and boiled in the same way. Instead of drying it, the Welsh have always preferred to cook their laver, boiling it for up to six hours into a mucilaginous seaweed porridge, dark green and delicious. The seaweed became thicker as it boiled and required frequent stirring with long paddles, coming to feel like one was 'rowing across the sea', as one old gatherer described it.

After cooking, the women took the cockles and laver to market or sold them door to door. People liked to buy and eat the two together, calling them an 'old meal', rooted in tradition. The combination is seen most often today in the 'Welsh breakfast', which should always include laver, often with cockles, customarily warmed in bacon fat. A second distinctive pairing involves another Welsh speciality, lamb. Wales is known for its lamb, and the best has always been reckoned to be salt marsh lamb, from lambs which graze on the marshes

Traditional Welsh breakfast with fresh laverbread on the left and, below, 'Welshman's caviar', dried laver, sprinkled over egg, Pembrokeshire Beach Food Company.

next to the estuaries where laver and cockles are gathered. Laver has long been used to make a sauce for roast salt marsh lamb, the marine savours of meat and sauce complementing each other perfectly.

Wales has its own version of the poverty myth, which maintains that laver was only a food for the families of the poor miners and factory workers who came to Wales in the nineteenth century, but seaweed is as ancient a food there as elsewhere in Britain. It was always remarked on by travellers to the area, as in this account from the 1772 edition of William Camden's *Britannica*: in Wales, he wrote, there was

> a sort of Food, made in several parts of the county, of a sea-plant . . . they gather a kind of Alga or seaweed, with which they make assort of food called Lhaven or Lhawvan, in English-black butter. Having gathered the weed, they wash it clean from sand and slime and

sweat it between two tile-stones, then they shred it small and knead it well, as they do for dough for bread, and make it up into great balls or rolls, which some eat raw and others fry'd with oatmeal and butter. It is accounted sovereign against all distempers of the liver and spleen . . .[19]

This method produces a firmer textured laver than the kind that is generally eaten in Wales today.[20]

In the twelfth century, the historian Gerald of Wales (Giraldus Cambrensis) said of Welsh cookery: 'the kitchen does not supply many dishes, nor high-seasoned incitements to eating.' Traditional Welsh food was the epitome of what used to be called 'plain cooking'; when it came to laver, they saw no reason to eat it any other way than on its own, simply stewed or boiled, except for one variation. When it is eaten on its own, it is simply 'laver' or *lawr*; when it is mixed with oatmeal, made into cakes and fried, it is called 'laverbread' (*bara lawr*), although the two terms are often used interchangeably today.

New seaweed snacks from the long-established Welsh laver and seafood firm Selwyn's Seaweed, based on the Gower Peninsula. The packaging shows the coastline of Swansea Bay, where the commercial cultivation of seaweed is being introduced.

For many of the older generation, laver is so much the emblematic food of Wales and the symbol of Welshness – 'as Welsh as our unspoilt rolling moorlands, mellifluous male voice choirs and long place names'[21] – that it has long been available tinned, and now vacuum-packed, so it can be enjoyed by those who have moved away. For many returnees, it is the first food they want to eat on coming home, and one that they make sure to take away with them when they leave. For that reason, it is sometimes called the 'weed of *hiraeth*', *hiraeth* being the Welsh word for the deep longing for home.[22]

Welsh laver is a good example of fashions in food. From the 1970s, laver eating declined among the young, who saw it as old-fashioned and provincial at a time when many were keen to promote Wales as modern and cosmopolitan. People became very diffident about the seaweed, wanting it to be known that Welsh cuisine was more than just lamb, leeks and

New uses of Welsh seaweed include laverbread pesto, Pembrokeshire Beach Food Company.

Tinned laverbread from Wales, by Parsons Pickles of Carmarthenshire.

laver. Happy to eat sushi when it was introduced, they declined to eat laver, even though it was the same kind of seaweed. But with the shift to natural foods and local produce, and a recognition of the value of *terroir* and culinary tourism, laver has come back into its own.

The industry is now thoroughly modernized, the commercial growing of laver on rafts in Swansea Bay is being developed and Welsh laver is exported as far as Japan, where it is relished by connoisseurs. In Wales, local chefs have broken through the conservatism of Welsh laver eating, and now produce a range of imaginative dishes, from laver soufflé to laver pesto for pasta, and there is a new range of seaweed snacks, salts and relishes. It also appears as an ingredient in *cawl lawr*, seaweed soup, an adaptation of Wales's hearty national soup, *cawl*; and there is seaweed gin, infused with handpicked seaweed. Firmly back at the centre of its culinary heritage, laver is Wales's new green-black gold.

Seaweed in England

Although England appears to have no tradition of eating sea-weed, in prehistory the usual practices would have been carried on along suitable stretches of the coast, and there are tantalizing hints of seaweed use in early historic times. Long-unspoken words preserved in *A Thesaurus of Old English*, which has five terms for seaweed, shows familiarity with its use as food and medicine,[23] as does this remedy from the Anglo-Saxon *Leechdoms* compiled in the tenth century, but drawing on earlier material: 'As liquid emetic . . . again pound iris, ground ivy, seaweed in ale, and then sweeten it to drink.'[24]

Medical use no doubt continued, although hidden behind catch-all terms such as *wyrt* (wort) or *weod* (weed), which obscure the difference between marine and land plants. Later, there are isolated glimpses of seaweed being consumed. In the eighteenth century, 'fine potted laver' was a street cry in Bath, sung out by enterprising Welsh vendors from the coast who travelled up to sell their healthy wares to people who had come to take the spa city's famous water cure.[25] In 1853 a writer on algae in Britain reported that on the northern British coasts dulse was

> carried to the markets of country towns, where it is sold and eaten with potatoes, sometimes being boiled but in many places eaten raw, just as it is gathered fresh from the sea. Cattle and sheep are especially fond of it, and the latter always eat it with avidity whenever they find their way to the rocks where it grows, or is cast ashore.[26]

Elsewhere, laver – there called 'black butter' and spread on bread – was eaten on the coasts of Devon, across the

'Black butter', or laver, served with toast.

Bristol Channel from Wales, as well as in Somerset, and laver was pickled and used as a relish in Cornwall.

In smart society, laver found an advocate in Eneas Sweetland Dallas, who in 1877 published *Kettner's Book of the Table*, writing of laver:

> Many an old-fashioned English gentleman will be glad to see laver mentioned here . . . It used to be common enough in London; now it is scarce, though there are clubs in Pall Mall and private families that never fail of it. That it should fall into neglect is one of the unfortunate results of modern civilization, which produces uniformity of fashion – the same cookery and the same dishes all over the world.

Undersea landscape from the *Brockhaus and Efron Encyclopedic Dictionary* (1890–1907).

Warming to his subject, Dallas pointed out that England, being nearly all seaboard, was at a great advantage, as were other parts of Britain:

> And here upon their seaboard the English can get any quantity of laver; on the coast of Scotland there is delicious dulse; in Ireland there is the carrageen or Irish moss. These and other seaweeds that might be named are wonderfully nutritious, are full of fine flavour, and are to be had for the gathering. If the French cooks had made their mark in England, would they have let the laver fall into disuse? They would have made it as famous as the truffles of Perigord.[27]

Charles Dickens was also a fan, writing that 'There is not a single poisonous seaweed, while many are nutritious and restorative. They render us enormous indirect service by affording pasture to legions of living creatures which supply food to fish, who are food for men.'[28] But on the whole, in England by the late nineteenth century, seaweeds had slipped from mainstream view, and the many Victorian and Edwardian cookbooks published for invalids who would greatly have benefited from the nutritious properties and digestibility of seaweeds do not mention them, with the exception of carrageen toddies or jellies, and those rarely. In Mrs Beeton's encyclopaedic *Book of Household Management*, seaweeds were dismissed in a few disdainful words:

> Seaweeds are occasionally employed as food. Irish moss, or carrageen, is given to consumptive patients, and is also used commonly as a food in some places. In 100 pounds of the moss there are only 19 of water and 9 of albuminoids so that it is among the most nourishing

'The Ocean's Gay Flowers': a traditional English seaweed-flower greetings card, late 19th century.

Flowers in a seaweed-pattern bowl, greeting card, late Victorian.

vegetable foods we have. Laver, tangle or red ware and pulse are also collected and eaten in pickle or as a substitute for other boiled vegetables.[29]

The English view of seaweed was captured in the popular poem 'From a Victorian Seaweed Picture':

Ah! Call us not Weeds but Flowers of the Sea
For lovely and gay and bright tinted are we
Our Blush is as bright as the Rose of thy Bowers
So call us not Weeds but the Ocean's gay Flowers.[30]

In the wake of the Victorian enthusiasm for natural history inspired by Charles Darwin, the English took up seaweed not as food but as art. Suddenly it was everywhere, found in seaweed embroideries and dried seaweed collages, watercolours and sketches of seaweed, either on its own or as part of picturesque seaside scenes and fanciful undersea landscapes. There were seaweed-patterned dress textiles and furnishing fabrics, seaweed wallpapers and greetings cards, seaweed jewellery and seaweed ceramics of all kinds, and from then until the present, seaweed has never gone out of fashion as an English art motif. The English still happily eat seaweed with their eyes – but resist swallowing it.

Seaweed in Scotland

Hunter-gatherers settled the west of Scotland by at least 6000 BC, sustained by the abundant coastal resources including seaweed, which were essential to their success and have been used ever since as food, medicine and fertilizer. Its ancient importance can be glimpsed in the survival into early modern times of pre-Christian rituals intended to secure a good harvest of seaweed or 'sea ware' in the coming year, among them a Hallow-tide (Samhain) ritual in honour of the Hebridean sea god Shony, observed by the traveller Martin Martin in the Isle of Lewis in 1703:

> one of their number was picked to wade into the sea up to his middle, and carrying a cup of ale in his hand, standing still in that posture, cried out with a loud voice saying 'Shony, I give you this cup of ale, hoping that you'll be so kind as to send us plenty of sea-ware for enriching our ground for the ensuing year', and so threw the cup of ale into the sea.[31]

On Iona, the man making the offering chanted in Gaelic as he waded into the sea:

O God of the Sea
Put weed in the drawing wave
To enrich the ground
To shower on us food.[32]

In other places, great cauldrons of porridge were poured into the sea as a gift to the ocean gods, in the hopes of procuring a rich sea harvest. The link between the two was clear – without the seaweed to fertilize the fields, the oats would not grow. Into the nineteenth century, supplications to the sea for an abundance of seaweed were still being made:

Green seaweed smoothie created by Xa Milne.

Shortbread sprinkled with Mara Shony seaweed.

> Come and come is seaweed,
> Come and come is red sea-ware,
> Come is yellow weed, come is tangle,
> Come is food which the wave enwraps.[33]

As in Ireland, the favoured edible seaweeds in Scotland are dulse and carrageen. Dulse was made into a thick broth with oatmeal (*càl duilisg*), boiled and buttered or stewed in butter, roasted in the fire and served up with vinegar or added to stews or ragouts to give them a red colour, and a thicker and richer consistency.[34] Other seaweeds eaten in Scotland include grockle, 'dabberlocks' (*Alaria esculenta*), sugar wrack consumed as snacks and sea tangle, a kind of kelp (*Laminaria digitata*), that was reported to be rather nice eaten raw after being dipped in whisky, and was also roasted to make a paste that could be spread on bread. Laver, called sloke here and in Ireland, also slabhagan, was eaten stewed with butter, sometimes flavoured with leeks or onion, something the Welsh would consider culinary heresy. An early account claimed that this was 'the only food that a human might need to survive' – possibly for this reason, Caithness fishermen took stewed sloke to eat while at sea.[35] In fashionable circles, sloke used to be highly esteemed as 'marine sauce'.[36] Sloke was also added to oatmeal to make flat bannocks.[37] Seaweed marries exceptionally well with oats, adding important nutrients to that starchy staple.

A dark chapter in seaweed's history in Scotland came with the Clearances, when landowners moved small farmers off the land to make way for sheep, 'putting people down on the beach to eat seaweed', as one descendant remembered.[38]

Dulse burgers made with dulse, beef and oyster sauce.

Yet when they emigrated in their numbers to Canada's Maritime provinces, they took their dulse-eating habits with them. In Scotland as elsewhere, the idea that seaweeds were only famine foods is disproved by the fact that they were eaten by choice in times of plenty.[39] In prosperous mid-Victorian Edinburgh, 'Wha'il buy dulse and tang!' was one of the cries of the fishwives in the streets,[40] while in Aberdeen at the same period 'dulse-wives' gathered in Castlegate to sell dulse and spicy pepper dulse (*Laurencia pinnatifida*), a highly regarded delicacy still sought after today. Although it was also enjoyed fried or toasted with hot irons, in Aberdeen dulse was generally eaten raw, and was considered an 'admirable' seasoning for oaten or wheaten bread and porridge, serving as the common breakfast relish of the Aberdonians. Dulse can also be mixed with meat to enhance the *umami* flavour of stews, meatloaf and burgers.

Compared to these rather refined urban uses, it was in the crofts of the western coasts and islands – a model of adaptation to the environment – that seaweed was seen at its most elemental, making the difference between life and death. Animals as well as people depended on seaweeds. The wracks could be boiled with oatmeal, husks or chaff to serve as winter fodder, or the animals would forage seaweed for themselves, like the famed sheep of North Ronaldsay and goats, sheep and deer elsewhere. Seaweed was dug into the poor, hilly land to sustain crops of oats, wheat, barley, potatoes, onions, turnips and brassicas, which formed the basis of croft cookery – simple stews and broths cooked in a large cauldron – to which dulse would have made a welcome addition.[41] Seaweed was also used in gardens, and was the basis of an extensive coastal pharmacopoeia of traditional remedies: linarich was applied to the temples to procure sleep and stop headaches and fevers; sea tangle restored appetite; dulse was

Focaccia made with Mara kombu seaweed.

effective against migraine, distemper and colic; and there were many other applications.[42] Seaweed could be burned for fuel when peat was not available or be made into dye for tweeds; the burned ashes of seaweed could be used to preserve food instead of salt and to bleach coarse linen; and it provided material for the soda, glass and iodine industries. It even served as a weather predictor – if a piece of seaweed hanging outside the front door went limp, it indicated that a storm was brewing. This was not due to magic, but to the fact that seaweed absorbs moisture from the air and so goes slack in the humidity that precedes rain.

Today, the traditional crofting lifestyle has disappeared, along with the additional income provided by the seaweed industry, with commercial firms who used to buy from

Scottish harvesters now preferring to take larger and cheaper consignments from elsewhere. However, with its cold and unpolluted waters, the Scottish coast and islands – notably the Hebrides – have become the home of many small producers who, drawing on local knowledge of an intensive interaction with seaweed over time, sell a wide range of dried seaweed and seaweed products to consumers around the world, to use in cookery and for other purposes.

Seaweed in Scandinavia

Lying north of Scotland and the British Isles, the islands and coasts of the Viking sphere have a long tradition of seaweed use. Iceland and the Faroe Islands were demanding environments, dependent on the rich marine resources of the North Atlantic kelp forests which surround them. In the now-familiar pattern, seaweed – fresh, dried, brined, smoked, pickled or fermented – was an important element in the diet. In the Faroe Islands dried seaweed was ground to make 'black salt', long the only form of salt available there; in Iceland, 'sol' (*Rhodymenia palmata*) was considered so important that collecting rights were set out in Iceland's oldest law book, written in the twelfth century.[43] The sol was consumed raw on the coast or dried and traded over long distances in exchange for wool and meat. It was eaten on a daily basis by rich and poor, with dried fish and butter or with milk and bread, and used as a cure for ailments such as nausea, indigestion and seasickness. *Alaria esculenta*, *Chondrus crispus* and *Gigartina mamillosa* were steeped in fresh water and then cooked with water or milk and flour to make a thick pudding eaten with milk or cream.[44]

A key moment in Iceland's great epic, the thirteenth-century *Egil's Saga*, turns on seaweed. In it, the hero Egil, grieving for

Seaweed in Balsfjord, Norway.

his dead son Bodvar, lost the will to live and refused food. His daughter, Thorgerd, tricked him into eating dulse, saying it was bad for him and would speed his death, but instead its nourishing qualities saved Egil, allowing him to recover from his bereavement. Seaweed did not save the Norse colonies in Greenland, but it was a valued provision on Viking voyages and an important part of the diet along the coasts of Scandinavia, where today it is central to an emergent cuisine which many see as the culinary future of seaweed.

In Europe, 'cultural appropriateness' has always been a challenge – if people do not want to eat the old-fashioned seaweed dishes of their homeland on the one hand or Asian food on the other, what is the alternative? An answer has presented itself in what is called the New Nordic Cuisine. Associated with the acclaimed Copenhagen restaurant Noma, the chef René Redzepi and the Nordic Food Lab, the movement has sought to create a new way of cooking and eating based on purity, freshness, simplicity and ethical principles. The movement encourages the eating and cooking of food that is seasonal, using local produce, developing new versions of Nordic foods and combining Nordic culinary traditions with influences from abroad in a very sophisticated manner.[45] In the New Nordic Cuisine, the rigour of the scientific laboratory meets the creativity of the chef's kitchen, using techniques such as cold-infusion and equipment like the Pacojet, which purées frozen foods, on high-quality ingredients chosen with attention to both taste and chemistry. Within Scandinavia, this has led to a revitalization of Nordic cuisine, including the imaginative use of local seaweed to produce Nordic dashi made with Scandinavian dulse rather than kombu, and seaweed prepared in other ways, resulting in dishes like: fresh cheese made of dulse-infused milk, dulse ice cream, savoury tarts with crunchy seaweed crusts, scallops on a bed of mixed grains with a sauce of squid ink and seaweed, and many more[46] – traditional foods made contemporary and culturally relevant. As the originators of the movement see it, the objective is not to reproduce Nordic eating internationally, but for other countries to develop their own culturally appropriate cuisines using the principles developed in Scandinavia, which could open new opportunities for seaweed eating around the world, building on the adaptability of seaweed.

Afterword:
The Future is Seaweed

In today's world, seaweed is not just for eating. Phycocolloids are as indispensible to the cosmetic and toiletries industries as they are to processed foods, and seaweed extracts are to be found in everything from lipstick and face creams to deodorants, shampoos and toothpaste, in both the mainstream and 'natural cosmetic' sectors. Seaweed is a component of foams, polishes and finishes of many kinds – from furniture-care cream and paints to dyes and fire-fighting foam. Seaweed is central to the search for greener and more eco-friendly plastic products, with seaweed-based bioplastics seen as a future source of stretchable and shrinkable films, adhesives and coatings. Seaweed in liquid or pellet form is a popular soil conditioner in gardens, following ancient usage, and is now being revived for commercial use to increase agricultural yield and improve the uptake of nutrients from the soil. Seaweed is also increasingly used as an additive to animal feed, especially for sheep and cattle. Claims are made by feed producers that seaweed additives in animal foodstuffs increase fertility, the quality of wool and the shininess of coats, improve nutrition and generally enhance vigour and health, augmenting immunity so that the use of antibiotics for animals can be lessened or dispensed with.

Phycocolloids are also used extensively in the pharmaceutical industry as a binder and emulsifier in pills, syrups, capsules, gels, suppositories, laxatives and ointments. Increasingly, medical researchers are investigating seaweeds for use in drug development, seeing them as a new source of biochemical materials with wide-ranging medicinal and other applications. Seaweed has long been used in traditional medicine in the East and in the West many seaweed 'therapies' are sold in the alternative and natural remedy sectors, but within established Western medicine the road from drug discovery and development through regulatory responsibilities to commercialization is a long and expensive one, so a mainstream medical 'seaweed pharmacy from the sea' remains in the future.

Most of all, scientific and industrial attention is being focused on seaweed as a future source of energy, as a replacement for fossil fuels. Commercial interest in seaweed goes up and down in direct proportion to concern about the supply of fossil fuels. In the 1970s there was a spike of interest, which died down again when the oil crisis of the day passed. Now, with concern about fossil fuel depletion again high, much effort is being spent on developing ways to extract energy from marine algae in two main ways: through extracting lipids to convert into biodiesel, and through extracting fermentable sugars to produce bioethanol. It is touted as 'green energy' by its promoters, who compare this fuel from the sea to oil without the pollution, but this remains to be proven. While it is possible to generate marine biofuels in laboratories on a small scale, it has so far proved difficult to scale up production to meet the needs of the world mass market for energy – one reason being that it is difficult to obtain sufficiently large quantities of seaweed. At present in the East, commercial efforts are focusing on seaweed farming to obtain supplies, while the West concentrates on wild harvesting, particularly of kelp. Both approaches seem to be environmentally friendly, but are frequently not. Coastal seaweed farming often requires clearing the seabed, destroying the original ecosystem, and can involve the importation of species which prove to be invasive. In the deep sea, overharvesting kelp destroys the marine life that depends on it.

Damage of this kind has already become apparent. Chile is an example of a country seeking alternative methods.[1] Another is Norway, where the introduction of mechanized harvesting of kelp for biomaterials has raised many ecological and ethical issues regarding the relative 'values' of commerce on the one hand, and the impact on the fish, sea mammals, birds, fishermen and marine ecosystem as a whole on the other.[2] Overall, a note of caution needs to be sounded. Although apparently beneficial in the short term, by further intensifying terrestrial cultivation and animal production, implementing intensive mechanized harvesting and supporting the prodigal use of energy, these projected uses of seaweed as biofuel and feedstock additives perpetuate a system that has already proved to be unsustainable, damaging to human health and to the terrestrial environment. We need to guard against the same thing happening to the sea. The need for ocean restoration, climate change mitigation and marine ecosystem protection is now urgent.[3]

Seaweed – Into the Blue

By comparison, the sustainable use of seaweed as food is positive, unproblematic and pleasant. A recent article in the *New Yorker* magazine began: 'seaweed could be a miracle food – if we can figure out how to make it taste good.'[4] Many delicious possibilities have been presented here. As seen in this brief edible history, seaweed has been a keystone food for humankind since earliest times, in the West as well as in the East. This book has mainly followed the great Kelp Highways because this is where the most ancient seaweed-eating cultures are to be found, and clear patterns have emerged. Two seaweeds have been particularly important in human history – kelp and *Porphyra*, of which it has been said that 'the human relationship with *Porphyra* (*Rhodophyta*) is perhaps closer than with any other alga.'[5] Traditionally, seaweed was never seen on its own but as part of a larger food web of fish, shellfish and sea mammals, and was valued as such. Nor was it eaten on its own – it has always been used as part of the larger diet, supplementing, balancing and optimizing it. As the seaweed expert David Myslabodski has said: 'What would be the health benefits to people in developing countries if just 3 percent of sea farina were added to the tortillas, pitas and breads of the world?'[6] And seaweed could have an equally beneficial effect on the over-nourished.

Seaweed was not just a coastal food, but was always a valuable commodity, traded inland over great distances. It was not a forage food freely available to all, but was regulated in law from earliest times. Far from being a famine harvest, it was often considered a food for the elite, only becoming more widely available in relatively recent times. In traditional diets, seaweed was used as a supplement, not a main food, so the quantities required to reap nutritional benefits did and do not place a strain on the environment. The age-old association between seaweed and shellfish has been seen worldwide, and demands further investigation and development for nutritional, environmental and conservation reasons. There are traditional uses of seaweed in many parts of the world, including the southern Atlantic coast of Europe, West Africa, Southeast Asia and

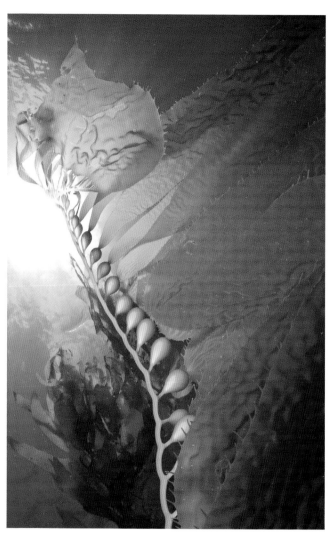

Drifting kelp.

South and Central America, that need to be recorded, and new sustainable uses of seaweed encouraged everywhere.

Supremely adaptable, seaweed accommodates all kinds of cuisines and cookery techniques, and can be either a prominent ingredient or one that imparts its benefits invisibly – boons established over aeons of consumption, now given scientific validation. Indeed, science has discovered seaweed, taking it from a niche area of marine botany to a rapidly developing field, driven by the interests outlined above, in just a few years. And yet, lurking behind the science are the older folklore and myths that bespeak the otherworldly fascination that seaweed has always exercised. In Japan, Korea and China there is a legend about an island of women in the cold kelp seas.[7] The women lived in dwellings thatched with seaweed, ate only fish and seaweed, and became pregnant by plunging into the sea. Some said they were human, some seals, some both. Similar myths can be found around the world, notably the selkies of the silver Celtic and Nordic seas who, when they come ashore in human form, eat seaweed soup. Growing between land and sea, past and future, seaweed is the ocean's great gift, offering unique benefits to us and our planet. It is time to plunge into the Blue.

Recipes

Highly adaptable to many ways of cooking, seaweed is also extremely variable, depending on type, season of gathering, location of origin, and method of processing, so there is no 'right' way to cook it, but many options. This is where producers' recipes are of great practical help, because they have been developed to make use of particular products. As with all cookery, the best way to proceed is with an adventurous spirit, experimenting and discovering as you go; never stop looking for new recipes and cookbooks. The possibilities before you are as wide and deep as the sea itself.

Dried and vacuum-packed seaweeds from specialist producers are increasingly available to purchase via the Internet. Producers' websites, the Internet and blogs are excellent places to find recipes, and there is a growing list of specialist seaweed cookery books. See Select Bibliography and Websites and Associations on the following pages. With that in mind, the recipes presented here are historical curiosities or from hard-to-find sources, or personal favourites.

Seaweed soups are a universal dish, so a number have been included here for the sake of comparison, and the traditional association of seaweed and shellfish has also been highlighted. In the West, adding seaweed to bread is a popular and culturally relevant option, so several recipes have been given.

Dr Landsborough's Victorian Carrageen Toddy for Invalids
from Charles Dickens, ed., *Household Words* (1856)

The recipe is almost identical to that used to make aphrodisiac Irish Moss Punch in the Caribbean, the only difference being that in the Caribbean the preparation is taken as a syrupy liquid rather than as a set gel, and sometimes has rum added.

A teacup full of dried carrageen is boiled in water; this water, being strained, is boiled with milk and sugar and seasoning, such as nutmeg, cinnamon or essence of lemon. It is then put into a shape in which it consolidates like blancmange and when eaten with cream it is so good that many a sweet-lipped little boy or girl would almost wish to be on the invalid list to get a share of it.

Laver in the Old-Fashioned English Manner

By 1877, when Eneas Sweetland Dallas published *Kettner's Book of the Table* in London, laver was rarely eaten in England, which he much regretted, writing 'There is a charm about the weed which ought to have kept it in the front as one of the distinctions of English cookery.' Here is his simple recipe:

To prepare the laver, steep it in water to reduce the salt. Sometimes a little carbonate of soda is added, to take away bitterness. It is then stewed in water till it becomes tender, and can be worked like spinach with broth or with milk or with a pat of butter and a squeeze or two of lemon juice.

Smoked Mackerel Pâté with Laver

The best smoked mackerel pâté I know, from Colin Pressdee's *Welsh Coastal Cookery* (1995), a pioneering work on coastal cuisine.

450 g (1 lb) smoked mackerel, skinned and boned
2 tbsp horseradish sauce, hot or mild to taste
225 g (8 oz) low-fat curd or cream cheese
50 g (2 oz) fresh wholemeal breadcrumbs
1 tsp ground black pepper (or use peppered mackerel)
50 g (2 oz) prepared laver (Welsh, fresh or tinned/vacuum-packed, not dried)
juice of 1 lemon

Remove all skin and bones. Fork the flesh in a bowl or pound in a food processor for a few seconds. Add the cheese, horseradish sauce, breadcrumbs, laver, lemon juice and pepper, if using, and mix to a smooth paste. Chill for a minimum of two hours, preferably overnight so the flavours can blend.

Breton Seaweed Butter

This is a good example of something that can be made quickly and easily, but which transforms the taste of fish and shellfish, either used in cooking or spread on bread as an accompaniment. In Scotland, a similar butter is made using only dulse.

250 g (9 oz) butter (unsalted or salted, to taste) at room temperature
1 tbsp dried seaweed, mixed – wakame, fucus and nori or as liked – measured before reconstituting
sea salt, to taste

Reconstitute the seaweed by soaking in water, then pat completely dry. Mince finely and mix into the softened butter along with the salt. Chill for at least two hours to allow the flavours to blend. The amount of seaweed used can be increased according to taste.

Laver and Orange Sauce for Roast Mutton

This recipe is from the food historian Laura Mason, and appeared in her book *The National Trust Farmhouse Cookbook* (2009). It is, she says, the best recipe for laver.

450 g (1 lb) prepared laver
80 g (3 oz) butter
juice of 1 Seville orange (if not in season, use lemon or
tangerine juice)
salt and pepper

Heat the laver gently with the butter and season to taste with orange juice, salt and pepper. Serve very hot.

Dulse Soda Scones

These delicious scones come from Regina Sexton's *A Little History of Irish Food* (1998). They are, she writes, ideal when lightly toasted and served with creamy scrambled eggs. This recipe makes a baker's dozen.

10 g (½ oz) dried dulse
450 g (1 lb) plain white flour
1 tsp bicarbonate of soda (bread soda)
1 tsp salt
350–75 ml (12–13 fl. oz) buttermilk
1 egg, beaten

Preheat the oven to 200°c (400°F), leaving a floured baking tray in the oven to heat.

Soak the dulse in water for five minutes. Discard the water and chop the dulse into fine strips. Sieve the flour, bicarbonate of soda and salt into a large cool mixing bowl. Once sieved, run the dry ingredients through your fingers for a few seconds to aerate. Add the chopped dulse. Make a well in the centre and pour in most of the buttermilk. Steadying the bowl with one hand, work in a circular fashion with your other hand to draw the dry ingredients into the milk. Keep working in this fashion until the dough comes together. If you find the dough is a little stiff, then add the remainder of the buttermilk. The dough should feel light and pliable.

On a lightly floured surface, work the dough gently into a round shape, about 2.5 cm (1 in.) thick, with the palm of your hand. Brush lightly with the beaten egg and cut into scones. Place on the heated baking tray and bake in the preheated oven for 20–25 minutes.

Icelandic Dulse and Moss Bread

From Nanna Rögnvaldardóttir's *Icelandic Food and Cookery* (2001) comes this bread which combines lichen and seaweed, reflecting its landscape of origin. The recipe, she says, is not old, but both Iceland moss (*Cetraria islandica*, available in health food shops and from suppliers) and dulse were often added to bread in earlier times for their nutritional benefits. No extra salt should be needed, because the dulse is salty enough.

2 tbsp dry yeast

1 tsp sugar

2 cups lukewarm water

1 cup wholewheat flour

1 cup soaked, packed Iceland moss

½ cup chopped dulse

3 tbsp butter

3 cups bread flour or as needed

Dissolve the yeast and sugar in lukewarm water and let it stand until frothy. Stir in the wholewheat flour, cover and let the sponge rise in a warm place for fifteen minutes or so. Meanwhile, finely chop the Iceland moss and the dulse. The Iceland moss can be chopped in a food processor but the dulse preferably should be cut with scissors.

Melt the butter and let it cool slightly, then mix it along with the lichen and the dulse into the sponge. Gradually stir in enough bread flour to make a soft but workable dough. Knead it thoroughly, then shape it into a ball, place it in a bowl, cover loosely and let it rise at room temperature for an hour or so, or until doubled. Punch the dough down, knead it slightly and shape it into two loaves. Let them rise on a buttered and floured baking sheet for 25–30 minutes. Preheat the oven to 400°F (200°C). With a sharp knife, make diagonal slashes at 1-inch intervals on the surface of each loaf. Brush them with cold water and bake for around thirty minutes, or until they are golden and a hollow sound is heard when the bottom is tapped. Let them cool completely before cutting.

Julie's Crispbread with Seaweeds

This recipe for crispbread enriched with seaweeds and seeds comes from the scientist and seaweed historian Ole G. Mouritsen, and appears in his wonderful book *Seaweeds: Edible, Available and Sustainable* (2013).

150 ml rolled oats
150 ml flaxseed
100 ml sunflower seed
100 ml pumpkin seed
2 tsp salt
250 ml flour
1 tsp baking powder
4 tbsp mixed seaweed granules (sea lettuce, dulse, bullwhip kelp, giant kelp, *mekabu*)
200 ml water
2 tbsp grapeseed oil

In a bowl, mix together the oats, seeds, seaweeds, salt, flour and baking powder. Add water and mix well until the dough becomes sticky. Divide the dough into two and place one part on a piece of baking paper. On top of the dough add another piece of baking paper and roll the dough out evenly and as thinly as possible between the two. With a knife or pizza wheel, cut the top baking paper and divide the dough into squares without cutting through the bottom paper. Remove the top baking paper and place the dough and the bottom paper on a baking sheet. Repeat the procedure with the other part of the dough. Bake the crispbread at 200°C (400°F) for about fifteen to twenty minutes until the bread is golden brown. Let the crispbread cool on a baking rack. After a few minutes the crispbread can be broken along the scored lines.

Clams with Seaweed

This is a traditional recipe of the Kwakiutl people of the Pacific Northwest Coast, collected by the anthropologist Franz Boas, and included in his *Ethnology of the Kwakiutl* (1921).

Four large clams are taken and are opened. Then the sand is picked off; and when it is all off, they are put into the kettle. When this is done, water is poured on, but not very much water. The woman takes with her hands the meat of the cleaned clams and squeezes it, and she only stops squeezing it when the water is quite milky. Then she puts the kettle over the fire, and she lets it boil a long time. Then she pours oil into it. When this is done, she takes it off the fire. Then she pours cold water into it, until the kettle is more than half full. Then she takes chopped seaweed and puts it in, and she stirs it until it is the right thickness, and she puts the kettle back on the fire and she lets it boil for a long time, and she puts more oil into it. Then she takes the kettle off the fire, and it is done; and it is only eaten with spoons.

Spam *Musube*

A recipe from Hawaii, this is the most curiously delicious of nori-wrapped foods. Originated by the islands' Japanese community, but now eaten by everyone, Spam *musube* is a tasty alternative to the kind of sushi that takes itself too seriously.

1 can Spam
600 g (3 cups) uncooked sushi rice
sheets of nori as needed
3 tbsp soy sauce
3 tbsp sugar
furikake

Cook the rice and set aside to cool to room temperature. Slice the Spam into six to eight slices. Fry the slices, and pour over the sugar-soy sauce while frying, so it caramelizes. In the old days, one would dip one's hands into salted water, shape a handful of rice into a triangular cake with flat top and bottom, place a slice of the fried Spam on top, and complete with a strip of nori around the rice and Spam. A variation was to enclose the slice of fried Spam in rice, making a flat saucer-shaped cake, which was then covered completely in nori. A new way of making Spam musube involves the use of a moulding-box (*ashiwaku*) or '*musube*-maker' – a small box in which layers of cooked rice, then Spam and finally more rice are pressed firmly into a small block, which is then sprinkled with *furikake* – a Japanese condiment for sprinking over rice, consisting of ground seaweed, ground bonito flakes and sesame seeds – and wrapped in nori.
Makes 6 to 8 musube

Sukiyaki

Sukiyaki is a modern version of the ancient Japanese technique of one-pot cookery (*nabemono*). The interesting feature of this dish is that it was often cooked at the table in front of the guests, thus providing entertainment as well as a meal. People took what they wanted out of the pot, putting it on small dishes. Great pains were taken with the artistic arrangement of the raw ingredients on a large platter, placed so that they could be added at different stages in the cooking. *Sukiyaki* using beef became popular after the prohibition against meat-eating was discontinued in the nineteenth century. In the early years of East–West culinary encounters, *sukiyaki* was a dish that Westerners took to with enthusiasm.

1 ½ lb beef, sliced bacon-thin
10 green onions
2 bunches *shirataki* (long *konnyaku)* – 1 ½ cups
of sliced mushrooms may be substituted
⅔ lb *shungiku* (edible chrysanthemum leaves)
or bak choi cabbage
2 squares of broiled soy bean curd (tofu)
⅔ lb bamboo shoots
1 tbsp vegetable oil
⅔ cup soy sauce
8 tbsp sugar
2 cups water, to make soup stock
25 cm (10 in.) kombu seaweed
(used for seasoning soup stock only)
one egg per person

Mix the water and kombu seaweed to make the soup stock and allow to stand for about ten hours. Add the soy sauce and sugar, bring to a boil, remove from heat and strain.

Cut the green onions slantingly into about 5 mm (¼ in.) pieces. Wash the edible chrysanthemum leaves or bak choi thoroughly. Drain, wash and cut the *shirataki* into about 8 cm (3 in.) bits. Cut the broiled soy bean curd into twelve squares. Cut the bamboo shoots into thin pieces by cutting crosswise. Arrange the vegetables colourfully on a large platter.

Put the oil into the skillet; when it is hot, add some of each vegetable, starting with those that take the longest to cook, and brown them. Add some of the meat on top of the vegetables and add the soup stock. Last of all, add the *shirataki* and soy bean curd. Do not put all of the foods in at once. Adjust seasoning to taste by adding more soy sauce or sugar. This is to be eaten as it is cooked, and more food added when there is room in the skillet.

Allow one egg per person when serving. Individuals will put the hot *sukiyaki* into their bowls, then break the raw egg on top of it and eat with rice.

Dashi and *Suimono*: Egg Soup

From Aya Kagawa's *Japanese Cookbook* (1949), a volume intended to introduce Westerners to Japanese cookery and culinary culture. This passage describes *suimono* – clear soups – in a two-step process that begins with making the *dashi* or stock.

Both *katsuobushi* (a piece of dried bonito) and kombu or dried tangle are used. The best *katsuobushi* is called *tosa-bushi*, made at Tosa in Shikoku. To make dashi, *katsuobushi* is shaved. It is easier to shave after warming a little at the fire. For one person, about a tablespoonful of *katsuobushi* shavings is sufficient. The tangle is a kind of kelp produced chiefly in Hokkaido. It is cut into small pieces and used. For six persons:

½ cup *katsuobushi* shavings

1 square inch tangle

¼ tsp seasoning powder (MSG)

5 cups water

Put the tangle in water and boil. When large bubbles appear, take out tangle and put in shaved *katsuobushi*. When water reaches boiling point, take off fire. When the *katsuobushi* sinks, use upper clear liquid as stock. This is first *dashi*.

For second *dashi*, put 340 ml (1½ cups) of water in remainder of first *dashi*; put in used tangle and boil for 10 minutes; use as foundation for miso soup and boiled foods.

Egg Soup

2 eggs

1 piece nori

5 cups first *dashi*

2 tsp cornstarch

2 tsp salt

2 tsp soy

Put the *dashi* in a pot, heat and add liquid mixture of salt, soy and cornstarch. Beat the eggs in a bowl; when the soup boils, spread the eggs on the surface of the soup with a dipper with holes in it, as quickly as possible. The egg will float like threads on the soup. Add seasoned laver (nori) crushed or cut in little squares.

Okinawa Longevity Soup

One of the many Okinawan 'longevity soups', starting with a hearty pork stock that is skimmed several times to remove excess fat. The stock is then used as a basis for the soup. The Japanese influence can be seen in the use of bonito, the Chinese in the use of pork and the long-simmering technique.

900 g (2 lb) pork bones

225 g (½ lb) belly of pork

3.6 litres (3 quarts) water

1 ½ cups dried bonito flakes

1 tsp salt

1 tsp soy

Cover the bones and belly pork with water, bring to full boil, drain and rinse. Put water into pot, add bones and belly pork, bring to boil, cover and simmer for an hour, skimming off foam several times. Remove the meat and bones and set aside, strain stock and return to pot. Add flaked bonito to the pork broth, boil for two minutes, strain out the bonito, return the pork-bonito broth to the pot and add salt and soy. Make sure all the fat has been removed from the stock and from the cooked meat. Remove bones and cartilage and cut pork into pieces. Set aside. Meanwhile prepare:

6–8 dried shiitake mushrooms, quartered

1 piece dried konbu, about 15 × 20 cm (6 × 8 in.)

350 g (12 oz) white radish (daikon)
225 g (8 oz) mustard greens
5 cm (2 in.) piece of ginger root

Soak the dried konbu for half an hour or until pliable, cut into strips 1 cm by 2.5 cm (½ in. × 1 in.) and reserve. Cut mustard greens into strips 1 cm by 2.5 cm (½ in. × 1 in.) and reserve. Cut daikon into pieces of the same size, and reserve.

Add the mushrooms, ginger and konbu to the stock, bring to the boil, reduce the heat, add sliced pork and simmer for half an hour; add the konbu and daikon, then simmer for another fifteen minutes. Add additional soy and salt to taste, and then add the mustard greens at the end, cooking only briefly so they retain their colour and texture.

Filipino Clam and Seaweed Soup

The Philippines are one of the world's largest producers of the *Eucheuma* seaweeds, from which carrageen is extracted for industrial use. For local consumption, as in Hawaii, tropical seaweeds are often eaten fresh rather than dried. *Bagoong* is a pungent fermented fish paste. Asian fish sauce can be substituted for a lighter soup. Note the use of the water previously used for washing rice.

2 tbsp cooking oil
1 tsp minced garlic
2 tbsp chopped onions
3 tbsp *bagoong* sauce
1 tsp salt
900 ml (4 cups) of the cloudy water in which rice has been washed
90 g (½ cup) tomatoes, sliced
5 cups clams in shell
2 bunches fresh spinach
200 g (1 cup) seaweeds, cut 5 cm (2 in.) long (*Sargassum nigrifolium*)

Sauté the garlic, onion, tomatoes and clams. Season with *bagoong* sauce and salt. Add the rice washing water. Let the soup boil, add spinach and seaweed. Cook for three minutes, serve hot.

Serves 6

Chinese Seaweed Soup (*Zicai Tang*)

6 cups basic chicken, pork or fish stock
1 tbsp dried shrimp, soaked to soften, water reserved
¼ lb ground pork
1 cup dried seaweed soaked, rinsed and chopped
2 tbsp chopped green onion
½ tsp sesame oil

Bring stock and water shrimp has been soaked in to boil. Add pork and simmer for ten minutes. Raise heat, add soaked seaweed, bring just to the boil then lower heat and simmer for ten minutes. Add green onion and sesame oil. As a variation, bean curd (tofu) cut into diced pieces can be added during the last five minutes of cooking.

Korean Seaweed and Shellfish Soup (*Miyeok*)

This version of the renowned Korean *miyeok* soup is from the art and food historian Gillian Riley. It is one of her favourites, and she notes that it was traditionally made with oysters.

100 g per person of:

mussels
clams
cooked shell-on prawns
raw tiger or giant prawns
coarsely chopped garlic to taste, say 1 fat clove per person
wakame seaweed, treated according to the package, but do not overcook or soak for too long

good home-made or bought fish stock
Korean sesame oil

Shell the raw and cooked prawns, add the shells and heads to the ingredients for the fish stock, and cook, without salt, to get a nice tasty brew. Scrub the shellfish clean. Heat a mild or tasteless oil in a pan, and add the chopped garlic; when it starts to get golden and fragrant add the mussels and a dash of dry white wine, cover and cook. When the mussels have opened strain into a bowl, keeping the liquid. Reserve the mussels. Put the liquid back in the pan and cook the clams, strain, reserve them, and add the liquid to the pot, along with the juice from the mussels. Pour in some of your fish stock and add the seaweed, and let it soak a while but not too much or it will get soggy. Take the mussels and clams from their shells and tip into the pot, add the shelled prawns, heat gently for a very short time, add a few drops of Korean sesame oil, and serve.

Welsh Seaweed Soup (Cawl Lawr)

Cawl is the national soup of Wales, a hearty broth with vegetables and meat. There were regional variations, and this one made with laver is a coastal speciality. The basic stock is made with bacon, beef or mutton; fish or vegetarian stock can also be used.

2 litres (4 pints) stock
100 g (4 oz) carrots, chopped
225 g (8 oz) leeks, chopped
225 g (8 oz) potatoes, chopped
175 g (6 oz) Welsh laver, tinned or vacuum-packed

Sauté the vegetables until lightly browned, add stock and Welsh laver, preferably fresh or tinned/vacuum-packed. Simmer for twenty minutes, add seasoning of Welsh Halen Môn salt and serve.

References

Introduction

1 See wwf.panda.org, accessed June 2015.
2 Charles Darwin, *The Voyage of the Beagle* (London, 1845),
   p. 117.
3 See Global Seaweed Network, Natural History Museum,
   www.nhm.ac.uk, accessed June 2015
4 The Aquatic Biome, www.ucmp.berkeley.edu, accessed
   June 2015. See also www.microbeworld.org, accessed
   June 2015.
5 The Seaweed Site, www.seaweed.ie, accessed June 2015;
   Global Seaweed Network, accessed June 2015. See also
   Global Seaweed Network, Natural History Museum,
   accessed June 2015.
6 Louis D. Druehl, 'Cultivated Edible Kelp', in *Algae and
   Human Affairs*, ed. Carole A. Lembi and J. Robert Waaland
   (Cambridge and New York, 1988), p. 120.
7 Juliet Brodie, George D. Fussey, Jo Wilbraham and Michael
   D. Guiry, 'From Sir Joseph Banks to the World's Seaweed
   Colloid Industry: The Discovery of Original Material and
   Typification of the Marine Red alga Gloiopeltis tenax',
   Journal of Applied Phycology, XXVII (2015), pp. 1535–40.
8 Jerry G. Lewis, Norman F. Stanley and G. Gordon Guist,
   'Commercial Production and Applications of Algal
   Hydrocolloids', in *Algae and Human Affairs*, p. 206.

9 See Vazhiyil Venugopal, *Marine Products for Healthcare: Functional and Bioactive Nutraceutical Compounds from the Ocean* (Boca Raton, FL, 2008), p. 319.

10 Ole G. Mouritsen, *Seaweeds: Edible, Available, and Sustainable* (Chicago, IL, and London, 2013), p. 52.

11 Linda Howard, 'Seaweed: Super-wise your Meals', *Naked Food Magazine*, 28 May 2013, http://nakedfoodmagazine.com.

12 Georgia M. Hart et al., 'Contemporary Gathering Practice and Antioxidant Benefit of Wild Seaweeds in Hawai'i', *Economic Botany*, LXVIII/1 (2014), pp. 30–43 (p. 31).

13 S. N. Lim, P.C.K. Cheung, V.E.C. Ooi and P. O. Ang, 'Evaluation of Antioxidative Activity from a Seaweed, *Sargassum siliquastrum*', *Journal of Agricultural and Food Chemistry*, L (2002), pp. 3862–6.

14 Mouritsen, *Seaweed*, pp. 54–5.

15 Seibin Arasaki and Teruko Arasaki, *Vegetables from the Sea* (Tokyo, 1983), p. 46.

16 John Harvey Kellogg, *The Battle Creek Sanitarium System* (London, 1908), p. 151.

17 H. McGee, *On Food and Cooking: The Science and Lore of the Kitchen* (New York, 2007), p. 344.

18 Heston Blumental et al., *Dashi and Umami: The Heart of Japanese Cuisine* (London, 2009); O. G. Mouritsen et al., 'Seaweeds for Umami Flavor in the New Nordic Cuisine', *Flavour*, 1/4 (2012).

1 The Beginnings: Hiding in Plain Sight

1 Ole G. Mouritsen, *Seaweeds: Edible, Available and Sustainable* (Chicago, IL, and London, 2013), p. 2.

2 Karen Hardy et al., 'The Importance of Dietary Carbohydrate in Human Evolution', *Quarterly Review of Biology*, XC/3 (September 2015), pp. 251–68.

3 Tom D. Dillehay et al., 'Monte Verde: Seaweed, Food, Medicine, and the Peopling of South America', *Science*, CCCXX/5877 (9 May 2008), pp. 784–6.

4 Jon M. Erlandson et al., 'The Kelp Highway Hypothesis: Marine Ecology, the Coastal Migration Theory and the Peopling of the Americas', *Journal of Island and Coastal Archaeology*, II (2007), p. 171.

5 Ida Torres, 'Jomon Cuisine: What Went Into the Jomon Pots?', *Japan Daily Press*, 11 April 2013.

6 See Barry Cunliffe, *Facing the Ocean: The Atlantic and its Peoples, 8000 BC to AD 1500* (Oxford and New York, 2001).

7 M. Hodnett, 'The Sea in Roman Poetry', *Classical Journal*, XV/2 (1919), pp. 67–82.

8 Peregrine Horden and Nicholas Purcell, *The Corrupting Sea* (London, 2000).

9 In G. Irby-Massie and P. T. Keyser, *Greek Science of the Hellenistic Era: A Sourcebook* (London and New York, 2002), p. 259.

10 Hassan S. Khalilieh and Areen Boulos, 'A Glimpse on the Uses of Seaweeds in Islamic Science and Daily Life during the Classical Period', *Arabic Sciences and Philosophy*, XVI (2006), pp. 91–101.

11 Ibid., p. 100.

12 Richard Russell in the *Brighton Gleaner*, 1/5 (17 June 1822), p. 161.

13 See Anna Hunter, 'Seaweed: The Superfood for Skin, Hair and Health', www.getthegloss.com, 12 September 2013.

2 Seaweed in Japan

1 A. Okazaki, *Seaweeds and Their Uses in Japan* (Tokyo, 1971), p. 16.

2 Satori Horai et al., 'mtDNA Polymorphism in East Asian Populations, with Special Reference to the Peopling of Japan', *American Society of Human Genetics*, LIX (1996), pp. 579–90.

3 Bruce L. Batten, 'Provincial Administration in Early Japan: From Ritsuryo kokka to Ocho kokka', *Harvard Journal of Asiatic Studies*, LIII/1 (June 1993), pp. 103–34.

4 Edwin A. Cranston, 'The Dark Path: Images of Longing in Japanese Love Poetry', *Harvard Journal of Asiatic Studies*, xxxv (1975), pp. 60–100, p. 62.

5 J. L. Pierson, trans. and annot., *The Manyoshu* (Leiden, 1933), vol. III, poem 433, p. 293.

6 Cranston. 'The Dark Path', p. 65.

7 Ibid., p. 95.

8 Edwin O. Reischauer, 'The Izayoi Nikki, 1277–1280', *Harvard Journal of Asiatic Studies*, x/3–4 (December 1947), pp. 255–387, p. 307.

9 Anon., *1,000 Poems from the Manyoshu* (Tokyo, 2005), p. 191.

10 Joan R. Piggott, 'Mokkan: Wooden Documents from the Nara Period', *Monumenta Nipponica*, xLv/4 (1990), pp. 449–70, pp. 453, 458.

11 Kaori O'Connor, *The Never-ending Feast: The Anthropology and Archaeology of Feasting* (London, 2014).

12 D. L. Philippi, *Norito: A New Translation of Ancient Japanese Ritual Prayers. The Institute for Japanese Culture and Classics* (Tokyo, 1959), p. 32.

13 Helen C. MacCulloch, 'Aristocratic Culture', in *The Cambridge History of Japan*, vol. II: *Heian Japan*, ed. John Whitney Hall, Donald H. Shively and William H. McCulloch (Cambridge, 1999), pp. 390–441.

14 M. Ishii, 'Food Byways: Tracing the Old Kombu Route', *Food Forum*, xxvii/2 (2013).

15 Jonathan Deutsch, 'The Sumotori Diet', *Gastronomica*, I (Winter 2004), pp. 47–53.

16 Heston Blumenthal, Nobu Matsuhisa et al., *Dashi and Umami: The Heart of Japanese Cuisine* (London, 2009), p. 23.

17 Richard Hosking, *The Art of the Japanese Table* (Oxford and New York, 2000). See also Harold McGee, *On Food and Cooking: The Science and Lore of the Kitchen* (London, 2004), p. 342.

18 Ole G. Mouritsen and Klaus Styrbaek, *Umami: Unlocking the Secrets of the Fifth Taste* (New York, 2014).

19 B. Willcox, C. Willcox and M. Suzuki, *The Okinawa Way: How to Improve your Health and Longevity Dramatically* (London and New York, 2001).

20 S. Arasaki and T. Arasaki, *Vegetables from the Sea* (Tokyo, 1983), pp. 26–7.

21 Hosking, *The Art of the Japanese Table*, p. 19.

22 Etsuko Terasaki, 'Hatsushigure: A Linked Verse Series by Bashō and his Disciples', *Harvard Journal of Asiatic Studies*, XXXVI (1976), pp. 204–39, p. 220.

23 Hosking, *The Art of the Japanese Table*, p. 111.

24 Naomichi Ishige, *The History and Culture of Japanese Food* (London and New York, 2001).

25 S. Issenberg, *The Sushi Economy* (New York, 2007), p. 86.

26 T. Bestor, 'How Sushi Went Global', *Foreign Policy* (November/December 2001), pp. 54–63.

3 Seaweed in China and Korea

1 N. Silvin, *Traditional Medicine in Contemporary China* (Ann Arbor, MI, 1987); I. Veith, *The Yellow Emperor's Classic of Internal Medicine*, new edn (Berkeley, CA, and London, 1972), p. 21.

2 Silvin, *Traditional Medicine in Contemporary China*, p. 99.

3 Veith, *The Yellow Emperor's Classic of Internal Medicine*, p. 196.

4 Ibid., p. 199.

5 Eri Oshima, 'Medicinal Uses of Seaweed in Traditional Chinese Medicine', in *Traditional Chinese Medicine: Scientific Basis for its Use*, ed. E. Oshima, J. D. Adams and E. J. Lien (London, 2013), pp. 238–67.

6 Veith, *The Yellow Emperor's Classic of Internal Medicine*, p. 152.

7 Ibid., p. 23.

8 P. D. Buell and E. N. Anderson, *A Soup for the Qan* (London and New York, 2000), p. 196.

9 H. T. Huang, *Fermentations and Food Science*, part V of vol. VI: *Biology and Biological Technology*, the Joseph Needham Science and Civilization in China Series (Cambridge, 2000).

10 Ibid., p. 575.

11 Ibid., pp. 576–7.

12 Buell and Anderson, *A Soup for the Qan*, p. 433.

13 Chen Keji, ed., *Imperial Medicaments: Medical Prescriptions Written for Empress Dowager Cixi and Emperor Guangxu with Commentary* (Beijing, 1996), p. 270.

14 Lei Liu et al., 'Towards a Better Understanding of Medicinal Uses of the Brown Seaweed Sargassum in Traditional Chinese Medicine: A Phytochemical and Pharmacological review', *Journal of Ethnopharmacology*, CXLII (2012), pp. 591–619 (p. 615).

15 Buell and Anderson, *A Soup for the Qan*, p. 590.

16 W. M. Porterfield Jr, 'References to Algae in the Chinese Classics', *Bulletin of the Torrey Botanical Club*, XLIX (1922), pp. 339–40.

17 James Macaulay, ed., *The Leisure Hour* (August 1886), pp. 539–43 (p. 542).

18 B. Xia and I. A. Abbott, 'Edible Seaweeds of China and their Place in the Chinese Diet', *Economic Botany*, XLI/3 (1987), pp. 341–53.

19 'The Chinese Court at the Health Exhibition', *The Times* (London), 10 July 1884, p. 6.

20 Regional Council Hong Kong and the Palace Museum, Beijing, *Empress Dowager Cixi: Her Art of Living* (Hong Kong, 1996).

21 Ibid., p. 341.

22 I. J. Hodgkiss and K. Y. Lee, *Hong Kong Seaweed* (Hong Kong, 1983).

23 Xia and Abbott, 'Edible Seaweeds of China', p. 347.

24 Ibid.

25 Eric Tagliacozzo, 'A Necklace of Fins: Marine Goods Trading in Maritime Southeast Asia 1780–1860', *International Journal of Asian Studies*, I/1 (2004), pp. 23–48.

26 Frederick J. Simoons, *Food in China: A Cultural and Historical Inquiry* (Ann Arbor, MI, and Boston, MA, 1991), pp. 182–3.

27 Thomas O. Hollmann, *The Land of the Five Flavors: A Cultural History of Chinese Cuisine* (New York, 2014), p. 31.

28 Isabella Bird, *Korea and her Neighbours* (New York and Chicago, IL, 1898).

29 Michael J. Pettid, *Korean Cuisine: An Illustrated History* (London, 2008).

30 Okpyo Moon, 'Dining Elegance and Authenticity: Archaeology of Royal Court Cuisine in Korea', *Korea Journal* (spring 2010), pp. 36–59.

31 See Katarzyna J. Cwiertka, *Cuisine, Colonialism and Cold War* (London, 2012).

32 'Korean Food', www.korea.net, accessed 30 August 2015.

33 Pettid, *Korean Cuisine*, p. 25.

34 Richard Rutt, *The Bamboo Grove* (Ann Arbor, MI, 1971), p. 3.

35 David McCann, *Early Korean Literature* (New York, 2013), p. 28.

4 Seaweed in the Pacific and the Americas

1 Kaori O'Connor, 'The Hawaiian Luau: Food as Tradition, Transgression, Transformation and Travel', *Food, Culture and Society*, XXII/2 (June 2008), pp. 149–72.

2 Heather J. Fortner, *The Limu Eater: A Cookbook of Hawaiian Seaweed* (Honolulu, 1978), p. 40.

3 See 'Learning about Hawaii's Edible Seaweeds', http://manoa.hawaii.edu, accessed 22 August 2015.

4 Henry P. Judd, 'Hawaiian Proverbs and Riddles', *Bishop Museum Bulletin*, LXXVII (Honolulu, 1930), p. 75.

5 See http://manoa.hawaii.edu, accesssed 22 August 2015.

6 Vaughan MacCaughey, 'The Seaweeds of Hawaii', *American Journal of Botany*, III/8 (1916), pp. 474–9, p. 478.

7 Edith Kanaka'ole, 'Hi'ipoi i ka 'aina aloha', in *La'au Hawaii: Traditional Hawaiian Uses of Plants*, ed. Isabella Aiona Abbott (Honolulu, 1992), p. 45.

8 Fortner, *The Limu Eater*, p. 11.

9 Mary Kawena Pukui, 'Olelo No'eau: Hawaiian Proverbs and Poetrical Sayings', Bishop Museum Press Special Publication, no. 71 (Honolulu, 1983).

10 Fortner, *The Limu Eater*, pp. 28–9.

11 Ibid., p. 30.

12 Rudiger Joppien and Bernard Smith, *The Art of Captain Cook's Voyages*, vol. III (New Haven, CT, and London, 1988).

13 Hilary Stewart, *Indian Fishing: Early Methods on the Northwest Coast* (Seattle, WA, 1994), p. 18.

14 Ibid., p. 26.

15 Dino Labiste, 'Bull Whip Kelp', www.primitiveways.com, accessed 10 March 2016.

16 Nancy J. Turner and Helen Clifton, 'The Forest and the Seaweed: Gitga'at Seaweed, Traditional Ecological Knowledge and Community Survival', in *Eating and Healing: Traditional Food as Medicine*, ed. Andrew Pieroni and Lisa Leimar Price (New York and London, 2006).

17 Ibid., p. 163.

18 Ibid., pp. 164–5.

19 Frans Boas, *Ethnology of the Kwakiutl* (Washington, DC, 1921), pp. 292–6.

20 Kaj Birket-Smith, *The Chugach Eskimo* (Copenhagen, 1953), pp. 42–4.

21 Nancy J. Turner, 'The Ethnobotany of Edible Seaweed (*Porphyra abbottae* and related species: *Rhodophyta: Bangiales*) and its Use by First Nations of the Pacific Coast of Canada', *Canadian Journal of Botany*, LXXXI/4 (2003), pp. 283–93, p. 290.

22 J. Fisher, 'Notes on the Vapour Bath and its Variants', *Folklore*, lxii/3 (1951), pp. 367–82, p. 375.

23 Manuscript from the U.S./Canada Border Survey (1872), in the Christie Collection, British Museum. AOA dept bm, Notebook 30, Notes on record of NABC.

24 Turner, 'The Ethnobotany of Edible Seaweed', p. 286.

25 See *Camus: West Coast Cooking Nuu-cha-nulth style*, http://uuathluk.ca/wordpress/cookbook/; 'Indigenous Food Systems on Vancouver Island', http://mapping.uvic.ca, accessed 15 August 2015; and www.freshchoicekitchens.ca, accessed 15 August 2015. See also Andrew George and Robert Gairns, *A Feast for All Seasons: Traditional Native*

Peoples Cuisine (Vancouver, 2012), and Dolly and Annie Watts, *Where People Feast: An Indigenous Peoples' Cookbook* (Vancouver, 2007).

26 Margaret Denis Dubin and Sylvia Ross, *Seaweed, Salmon and Manzanita Cider: A California Indian Feast* (Berkeley, CA, 2008).

27 Eugenio Pereira Salas, *Apuntes para la historia de la cocina Chilena* (Santiago, 1977), English translation by James Stuart available at http://eatingchile.blogspot.co.uk, accessed 15 August 2015.

28 Ibid.

29 Sir Ernest Shackleton, *South! The Story of Shackleton's Last Expedition, 1914–1917* (London, 1919), p. 223.

30 William Wood, *New England's Prospect* [1639] (Boston, MA, 1865).

31 John Smith, *A Description of New England* (London, 1616), p. 30.

32 Michael J. Caduto and Joseph Bruchac, *Keepers of Life: Discovering Plants Through Native American Stories and Earth Activities for Children* (Golden, CO, 2000); see also Russell Peters and John Madama, *Clambake: A Wampanoag Tradition* (Los Angeles, CA, 1992).

33 Kathy Neustadt, *Clambake: The Celebration of an American Tradition* (Amherst, MA, 1992).

34 Yarmouth Branch of the Cape Cod Hospital Aid Association, 'How to Put on a Cape Cod Clam Bake' (Yarmouth Port, MA, 1949).

35 Hawk Hickok Hickman, *Knee Deep in Seaweed: Irish Sea Mossing in Scituate Mass in 1960–1997* (Scituate, 1997).

36 Marialisa Calta, 'New Brunswick's Sea Snack', *New York Times*, 6 September 1987.

37 Len Margaret, *Fish and Brewis, Toutens and Tales* (Canada's Atlantic Folklore – Folklife series) (St Johns, NL, 1980), p. 49.

5 Seaweed in Ireland, Wales, England, Scotland and Scandinavia

1 See E. J. Bean and T.P.S. Appleby, *Guidelines for Sustainable Intertidal Bait and Seaweed Collection in Wales: Legislative Review* (Bristol, 2014).

2 See Ole Mouritsen, *Seaweeds: Edible, Available and Sustainable* (Chicago, IL, 2013).

3 Elizabeth Field, 'Irish Seaweed Revisited', in *Wild Food: Proceedings of the Oxford Symposium on Food and Cookery* (Oxford, 2004), pp. 114–19.

4 Fergus Kelly, *A Guide to Early Irish Law* (Dublin, 1991), p. 107.

5 Lahney Preston-Matto, *Aislinge Meic Conglinne: The Vision of Mac Conglinne* (Syracuse, NY, 2010), p. 49.

6 Hugh Collins, 'Finger on the Dulse: The Rise of Northern Irish Seaweed', *Indie Farmer*, 21 August 2015, www.indiefarmer.com.

7 Heinrich Becker, *Seaweed Memories: In the Jaws of the Sea* (Dublin, 2000).

8 Ibid., p. 36.

9 Séamus Mac an Iomaire, *The Shores of Connemara* [1938] (Galway, 2000).

10 Collins, 'Finger on the Dulse'.

11 Mac an Iomaire, *The Shores of Connemara*, p. 167.

12 See Ole G. Mouritsen et al., 'On the Human Consumption of the Red Seaweed Dulse (*Palmaria palmate* (L), Weber & Mohr), *Journal of Applied Phycology*, xxv (2013), pp. 1777–91.

13 Regina Sexton, *A Little History of Irish Food* (London, 1998), p. 107.

14 Florence Irwin, *The Cookin' Woman: Irish Country Recipes* (Belfast, 1986), p. 196.

15 Mac an Iomaire, *The Shores of Connemara*, p. 169.

16 Sigerson Clifford, 'The Races', in *Ballads of a Bogman* (Cork, 1992). Crubeens are pig's trotters and Peg's Legs are sticks of rock candy. See Máirtín Mac Con Iomaire, 'Food as "Motif in the Irish Song Tradition"', http://arrow.dit.ie, accessed 20 August 2015.

17 First, Second and Third Drowned, in Dylan Thomas, *Under Milk Wood* (London, 1954).

18 J. Geraint Jenkins, *Cockles and Mussels: Aspects of Shellfish-gathering in Wales* (Cardiff, 1984).

19 A letter from the Reverend Mr Nicholas Roberts as quoted in Edmund Gibbon's 1772 edition of *Camden's Britannia*.

20 Bobby Freeman, *First Catch Your Peacock* (Talybont, 2006), p. 169.

21 Robin Turner, 'We Love Laverbread', *Western Mail* (Cardiff), 3 November 2004.

22 Kaori O'Connor, 'The Secret History of the Weed of Hiraeth: Laverbread, Identity and Museums in Wales', *Journal of Museum Ethnography*, 22 (December 2009).

23 Ann Hagan, *A Second Handbook of Anglo-Saxon Food and Drink: Production and Distribution* (Ely, 1999), p. 42.

24 Lch. II 268.8-9, in Noriko Unebe, 'Uses of Seaweed in Anglo-Saxon England: From an Ethnographic Angle', *Journal of Tokyo Kasei Gakuin University, Humanities and Social Sciences*, XLI (2001), pp. 85–94.

25 In Dorothy Hartley, *Food in England* (London, 2012), p. 284.

26 W. H. Grattan, *British Marine Algae* (London, 1853), p. 150.

27 Eneas Sweetland Dallas, *Kettner's Book of the Table* (London, 1877), pp. 272–3, https://archive.org, accessed 30 September 2015.

28 Charles Dickens, *All The Year Round*, vol. XVI (1 December 1866), p. 495.

29 *Mrs Beeton's Book of Household Management*, new edn (London, 1901), p. 728.

30 Hartley, *Food in England*, p. 285.

31 Martin Martin, *A Description of the Western Islands of Scotland* (1703).

32 Morgan Daimler, *Selected Prayers from Volume I of the Carmina Gadelica* (Raleigh, NC, 2011), p. 82.

33 From Alexander Carmichael's *Carmina Gadelica* (1997), a collection of poems, prayers and incantations from the Highlands during the last century. In Gregory Kenicer, Sam Bridgewater and William Milliken, 'The Ebb and Flow of

Scottish Seaweed Use', *Botanical Journal of Scotland*, LII/2 (2000), pp. 119–48, p. 131.

34 Kenicer et al., 'The Ebb and Flow of Scottish Seaweed Use', p. 121.

35 Martin, *A Description of the Western Islands of Scotland*, p. 148.

36 Marian McNeil, *The Scots Kitchen* (Edinburgh, 1929), p. 216.

37 Ibid., p. 121.

38 Leslie A. Robertson, *Imagining Difference: Legend, Curse and Spectacle in a Canadian Mining Town* (Vancouver, 2005), p. 49.

39 Kenicer et al., 'The Ebb and Flow of Scottish Seaweed Use', p. 120.

40 Charles Dickens, 'The Purple Shore', *Household Words*, vol. XIV (London, 1856), p. 319.

41 Kenicer et al., 'The Ebb and Flow of Scottish Seaweed Use', p. 126.

42 Martin, *A Description of the Western Islands of Scotland*, p. 148.

43 S. V. Hallson, *The Uses of Seaweeds in Iceland. Fourth International Seaweed Symposium* (Biarritz, 1961).

44 Ibid.

45 Nordic Food Lab, 'Beyond "New" Nordic', 18 May 2015, http://nordicfoodlab.org/blog/2015/5/18/beyond-new-nordic.

46 Ole G. Mouritsen et al., 'Seaweeds for Umami Flavour in the New Nordic Cuisine', *Flavour*, 1/4 (2012), www.flavourjournal.com, accessed 30 September 2015. This paper has recipes for dulse ice cream, fresh cheese with dulse and dulse bread, and gives a detailed insight into the kind of work undertaken by the Nordic Food Lab.

Afterword: The Future is Seaweed

1 Julio A. Vasquez, 'The Production, Use and Fate of Chilean Brown Seaweeds: Resources for a Sustainable Industry', *Nineteenth International Seaweed Symposium Proceedings* (2007), pp. 7–17. See also Celine Rebours,

Elaine Marinho-Soriano, Jose A. Zertuche-Gonzalez et al., 'Seaweeds: An Opportunity for Wealth and Sustainable Livelihood for Coastal Communities', *Journal of Applied Phycology*, XXVI/5 (2014), pp. 1939–51.

2 Sophia Efstathiou and Bjørn Myska, 'Weeding out the Sea: Adding "Value" to Norwegian Seaweed', paper given at 'Hidden Histories of Things/Commodity Histories', a workshop given at University College London, January 2015.

3 See www.greenwave.org.

4 Dana Goodyear, 'A New Leaf', *New Yorker*, 2 November 2015.

5 Thomas Mumford Jr and Akio Miura, 'Porphyra as Food: Cultivation and Economics', in *Algae and Human Affairs*, ed. Carole A. Lembi and J. Robert Waaland (Cambridge, 1989), p. 88.

6 FAO Prospects for seaweed in developing countries, Appendix A, www.fao.org/docrep/004/y3550e00.HTM (accessed 26 July 2016).

7 Carmen Blacker, 'Supernatural Abductions in Japanese Folklore', *Asian Folklore Studies*, XXVI/2 (1967), pp. 111–47.

Select Bibliography

Arasaki, Seibin, and Teruko Arasaki, *Vegetables from the Sea*
  (Tokyo, 1983)
Becker, Heinrich, *Seaweed Memories: In the Jaws of the Sea* (Dublin,
  2000)
Bird, Fiona, *Seaweed in the Kitchen* (London, 2015)
Blumenthal, Heston, with Nobu Matsuhisa, Kiyomi Mikuni and
  Pascal Barbot, *Dashi and Umami: The Heart of Japanese Cuisine*
  (London, 2009)
Bradford, Montse, and Peter Bradford, *Cooking with Sea Vegetables:
  A Vegan and Macrobiotic Cookbook* (London, 1985)
Dalrymple, Neil, *Gilgamesh* (The Gilgamesh Panels), www.
  neildalrymple.com
Dubin, Margaret Denise, and Sylvia Ross, *Seaweed, Salmon and
  Manzanita Cider: A California Indian Feast* (Berkeley, CA, 2008)
Ellis, Leslie, *Simply Seaweed* (London, 1998)
Erhart, Shep, and Leslie Cerier, *Sea Vegetable Celebration*
  (Summertown, TN, 2001)
Fortner, Heather J., *The Limu Eater: A Cookbook of Hawaiian
  Seaweed* (Honolulu, HI, 1978)
Gusman, Jill, *Vegetables from the Sea* (New York, 2003)
Hickman, Hawk Hickok, *Knee Deep in Seaweed: Irish Sea Mossing in
  Scituate, Mass., 1960–1997* (Scituate, MA, 2013)
— , *Seaweed Shanty Town* (Scituate, MA, 2016)
Lewallen, Eleanor, and John Lewallen, *Sea Vegetable Gourmet
  Cookbook and Wildcrafter's Guide* (Mendocino, CA, 1996)

Mac an Iomaire, Séamus, *The Shores of Connemara* (Galway, 2000)

McGee, Harold, *On Food and Cooking: The Science and Lore of the Kitchen* (New York, 2007)

Milne, Xa, *The Seaweed Cookbook* (London and New York, 2016)

Mouritsen, Ole G., *Seaweeds: Edible, Available and Sustainable* (Chicago, IL, and London, 2013)

—, *Sushi: Food for the Eye, Body and Soul* (New York, 2009)

—, 'The Emerging Science of Gastrophysics and its Application to the Algal Cuisine', *Flavour*, I/6 (2012)

—, and Klaus Styrbaek, *Umami: Unlocking the Secrets of the Fifth Taste* (New York, 2014)

—, Lars Williams, Rasmus Bjerregaard and Lars Duelund, 'Seaweeds for Umami Flavour in the New Nordic Cuisine', *Flavour*, I/4 (2012)

— , et al., 'On the Human Consumption of the Red Seaweed Dulse (*Palmaria palmata* (L) Weber & Mohr)', *Journal of Applied Phycology*, XXV (2013) pp. 1777–91

Pressdee, Colin, *Colin Pressdee's Welsh Coastal Cookery* (London, 1995)

Rhatigan, Prannie, *Irish Seaweed Kitchen* (Holywood, 2009)

Rhoads, Sharon Ann, with Patricia Zunic, *Cooking with Sea Vegetables* (Brookline, MA, 1978)

Rögnvaldardóttir, Nanna, *Icelandic Food and Cookery* (New York, 2002)

Sexton, Regina, *A Little History of Irish Food* (London, 1998), pp. 104–11

Tinellis, Claudine, ed., *Coastal Chef: Culinary Art of Seaweed and Algae in the 21st Century* (Madeira Park, BC, 2014)

Ulu-a-thluk (Nuu-chah-nulth) Tribal Council Fisheries Department, *Camus: West Coast Cooking Nuu-chah-nulth Style* (Los Angeles, CA, 2012)

Websites and Associations

I am not in favour of foraging. Traditional hunter-gatherer populations collected sustainably and responsibly for the good of their communities. Unfortunately, however well-intentioned they may be, modern amateur foragers acting individually tend to damage the marine and foreshore environments, as First Nations people have seen on the Pacific Northwest coast of North America and others are increasingly seeing elsewhere. My advice is to buy your supplies of seaweed from professional harvesters and suppliers like those listed below and visit their websites to read about what is involved in responsible and sustainable seaweed harvesting and use. Many producers' websites have recipes specially developed for their seaweeds and products.

America

http://dulseandrugosa.com

www.loveseaweed.com

www.naturespiritherbs.com

www.noamkelp.com (with recipes)

www.oceanapproved.com (with recipes)

www.oceanvegetables.com (with recipes)

www.ohsv.net (with recipes)

www.ryandrum.com/seaweeds.htm

www.seaveg.com/shop (with recipes)

www.seaweed.net (with recipes)

http://theseaweedman.com (with recipes)

www.vitaminseaseaweed.com/sea-vegetables (cookbook)

Canada
www.bckelp.com (with recipes)

www.canadiankelp.com/Blog.html

www.edibleseaweed.com (with recipes)

www.northpacifickelp.com

www.rolandsdulse.com (with recipes)

www.seaweedheaven.uk/Novia-Scotia

China
www.flavorandfortune.com (recipes only, search 'seaweed')

Cornwall and Channel Islands
http://cornishseaweed.co.uk (with recipes)

www.oceanharvest.je

England and Northern Ireland
http://abernethybuttercompany.com (dulse butter)

http://atlantickitchen.co.uk/seaweed (with recipes)

www.clearspring.co.uk (with recipes)

www.irishseaweeds.com (with recipes)

http://islanderseafood.com (with recipes)

www.seaveg.co.uk (with recipes)

Europe

www.algamar.com (with recipes)

www.algoplus-roscoff.fr (with recipes, in French)

www.algues-armorique.com (with recipes, in French)

www.algues.fr (with recipes, in French)

www.benboa.com (with recipes, in Spanish)

www.bord-a-bord.fr (with recipes)

www.portomuinos.com (with recipes)

www.suralgae.com (with recipes, in Spanish)

www.thalado.fr (with recipes, in French)

Ireland

www.blathnamara.ie (with recipes)

http://irishseaweedkitchen.ie (with recipes)

www.seaweedproducts.ie (with recipes)

Japan

www.ajinomotofoods.com (with recipes)

www.kikkoman.com (search for seaweed in the cookbook)

Scotland

www.hebrideanseaweed.co.uk (seaweed products)

www.ishga.co.uk (organic Scottish seaweed skincare)

www.justseaweed.com

http://maraseaweed.com (with recipes)

South America and Pacific

http://eatingchile.blogspot.co.uk (with recipes)

www.pacificharvest.co.nz (with recipes)

Wales

www.beachfood.co.uk (with recipes)

www.damhile.co.uk/shop/seaweed (seaweed gin, with recipes)

www.parsonspickles.co.uk (with recipes)

www.selwynsseaweed.com

Acknowledgements

Thanks are due to my editors Michael Leaman and Andy Smith, and to Martha Jay and Harry Gilonis of Reaktion Books. I am grateful to Gillian Riley and Helen Saberi for merry times and helpful suggestions beyond count; Timothy O'Sullivan for buoyant wit and wisdom; Noel Rees for boundless *hwyl* and supplies of laver; and to my daughter Kira Eva Tokiko Kalihilihiokekaiokanaloa Ffion Lusela Hopkins for being her wonderful self. Warm thanks are also due to Ole Mouritsen for his generosity and Susanne Højlund Pederson for her hospitality; the anthropologist James Stuart for the picture of Chilean seaweed; James Hamill of the Department of Africa, Oceania and the Americas, British Museum; the artist Neil Dalrymple for the Gilgamesh panel; Paul D. Barclay and the East Asia Image Collection, Lafayette College, PA; Colin Pressdee, Laura Mason, Regina Sexton and Nanna Rögnvaldardóttir for their recipes; Lyle Browning and other members of the Guild of Food Writers; New Brunswick Tourism; the Sitka Conservation Society; Ashley Jones and Selwyn's Seaweed, Parsons Pickles; The Pembrokeshire Beach Food Company; Xa Milne and Mara Seaweeds, Tom Crowley and the Hindu Kush Clothing Company, and the chef Cathal O'Malley's father. This book is dedicated to Peter Hopkins, *me ke aloha*.

Photo Acknowledgements

The author and publishers wish to express their thanks to the below sources of illustrative material and/or permission to reproduce it. Some locations of artworks are also given below.

Photo © adlifemarketing/iStock International Inc.: p. 107; photo Alexandar R.: p. 34; Archaeological Museum, Herakleion: p. 27; courtesy the author: pp. 31, 78, 87, 115, 117, 120, 122, 123, 132, 133; Bardo National Museum, Tunis: p. 29; Bibliteca Nacional de Madrid: p. 34; photo Botaurus: p. 37; from the *Brockhaus and Efron Encyclopedic Dictionary* (Leipzig & St Petersburg, 1890–1907): p. 130; photo © davelogan/iStock International Inc.: p. 96; photo © deeepblue/iStock International Inc.: p. 51; photo Diádoco: p. 129; photo © Ecopic/iStock International Inc.: p. 17; photo © Ezume-Images/iStock International Inc.: p. 74; from the Fine Arts Collection of the Cultural Group (Shansi province) under the State Council of the People's Republic of China: p. 77; photo © foodandwine photography/iStock International Inc.: p. 118; photo from the Freshwater and Marine Image Bank (http://digitalcollections.lib.washington.edu/cdm/search/collection/fishimages) at the University of Washington: p. 59; photo © Giovonni/iStock International Inc.: p. 88; photo © Deb Gleason/iStock International Inc.: p. 95; Bethany Goodrich/Sitka Conservation Society: p. 98; photo © hirophoto/iStock International Inc.: p. 60; photo Owen Howells: p. 124; from the *Illustrated London News*, 12 May 1883: p. 120; photos

Index

italic numbers refer to illustrations; **bold** to recipes